MW01078130

PRECIOUS TEACHERS

Also by Sangharakshita

Books on Buddhism
The Eternal Legacy
A Survey of Buddhism
The Ten Pillars of Buddhism
The Three Jewels

Edited Seminars and Lectures
The Bodhisattva Ideal
Buddha Mind
The Buddha's Noble Eightfold Path
The Buddha's Victory
Buddhism for Today – and Tomorrow
Creative Symbols of Tantric Buddhism
The Drama of Cosmic Enlightenment
The Essence of Zen
A Guide to the Buddhist Path
Human Enlightenment
The Inconceivable Emancipation
Know Your Mind
Living with Awareness
Living with Kindness
The Meaning of Conversion in Buddhism
New Currents in Western Buddhism
Ritual and Devotion in Buddhism
The Taste of Freedom
Tibetan Buddhism: An Introduction
Transforming Self and World
What Is the Dharma?
What Is the Sangha?
Who Is the Buddha?
Wisdom Beyond Words

Essays
Alternative Traditions
Crossing the Stream
Forty-Three Years Ago
From Genesis to the Diamond Sutra
The FWBO and 'Protestant Buddhism'
Going For Refuge
The History of My Going for Refuge
The Priceless Jewel
Was the Buddha a Bhikkhu?

Memoirs and Letters
Facing Mount Kanchenjunga
In the Sign of the Golden Wheel
Moving Against the Stream
The Rainbow Road
Travel Letters
Through Buddhist Eyes

Art and Poetry
The Call of the Forest and Other Poems
Complete Poems 1941–1994
In the Realm of the Lotus
The Religion of Art

Miscellaneous
Ambedkar and Buddhism
Peace is a Fire
A Stream of Stars

SANGHARAKSHITA

•

PRECIOUS TEACHERS

•

INDIAN MEMOIRS OF AN ENGLISH BUDDHIST

WINDHORSE PUBLICATIONS

Published by Windhorse Publications Ltd
11 Park Road
Moseley
Birmingham
B13 8AB

© Sangharakshita 2007
Cover design Dhammarati
All cover photographs © Clear Vision Trust Picture Archive,
except photo of Dudjom Rimpoche, courtesy Sangharakshita.
Printed by The Cromwell Press Ltd, Trowbridge, England

British Library Cataloguing in Publication Data
A catalogue record for this book is available from the British Library

ISBN 9781 899579 78 5

The right of Sangharakshita to be identified as the author of this work has been
asserted by him in accordance with the Copyright, Designs and Patents Act 1988

Contents

Photo Credits

BETWEEN PAGES 98 AND 99

All photographs © Clear Vision Picture Archive Trust
except Jamyang Khyentse Rimpoche, which is by courtesy of Sangharakshita,
from his private collection.

About the Author

SANGHARAKSHITA WAS BORN Dennis Lingwood in South London, in 1925. Largely self-educated, he developed an interest in the cultures and philosophies of the East early on, and realized that he was a Buddhist at the age of sixteen.

The Second World War took him, as a conscript, to India, where he stayed on to become the Buddhist monk Sangharakshita. After studying for some years under leading teachers from the major Buddhist traditions, he went on to teach and write extensively. He also played a key part in the revival of Buddhism in India, particularly through his work among followers of Dr B.R. Ambedkar.

After twenty years in India, he returned to England to establish the Friends of the Western Buddhist Order (FWBO) in 1967, and the Western Buddhist Order (called Trailokya Bauddha Mahasangha in India) in 1968. A translator between East and West, between the traditional world and the modern, between principles and practices, Sangharakshita brings to the task a depth of experience and clarity of thought that have been appreciated throughout the world. He has always particularly emphasized the decisive significance of commitment in the spiritual life, the paramount value of spiritual friendship and community, the link between religion and art, and the need for a 'new society' supportive of spiritual aspirations and ideals.

The FWBO is now an international Buddhist movement with over sixty centres on five continents. In recent years Sangharakshita has been handing on most of his responsibilities to his senior disciples in the Order. From his base in Birmingham, he is now focusing on personal contact with people.

PREFACE

During my years in India I had the good fortune to receive instruction and initiation from some the most eminent Buddhist teachers of their day. With one exception, I first met them in Kalimpong, a hill station in the state of West Bengal, thirty miles to the north-east of the bigger and better known hill station of Darjeeling.

Ranging in elevation from less than 4,000 feet at one point in the town to more than 5,600 in another, Kalimpong occupies the ridge between the Dailo and the Rinkingpong hills, high above the east bank of the River Teesta. A road runs along this ridge for some two to three miles, and from this road there straggle down the hillside the streets and lanes of the Kalimpong bazaar. The climate of the place is mild, the rainfall moderate, and for much of the year there is a fine view of the snows of Kanchenjunga and the other peaks of the eastern Himalayas.

I lived in Kalimpong from the spring of 1950 to the summer of 1964. At that time the population of the town and the surrounding hamlets must have been about 20,000. Besides the indigenous Lepchas, Bhutia, and Nepalese of various tribes and castes, it included people from many other parts of India and from several foreign countries. Kalimpong was thus a cosmopolitan and polyglot place, where any day of the year one could see a dozen different national and regional costumes and hear as many languages and dialects.

It was against the colourful background provided by this little hill station, which from the diversity of its religions and cultures well deserved its sobriquet of 'The Town of the Seven New Years', that I lived my life and first came into contact, especially during my last seven years there, with most of the teachers who are the principal subject of these memoirs.

I have sometimes been asked if among my teachers there was one who was spiritually more developed than the rest. A similar question was once put by a disciple to one of the members of the celebrated trio of spiritual masters that was made up of Chattrul Rimpoche, Jamyang Khyentse Rimpoche, and Dudjom Rimpoche, all of whom feature in the following pages. The master replied, 'One of us is indeed more spiritually developed than the others, but you disciples will never know which one it is.'

For my part, I have never tried to find out how my teachers compared with one another, spiritually speaking. Indeed, I never thought in such terms. It was enough that they were vastly superior to me in wisdom and compassion and that, by a strange combination of circumstances, I had come to be in contact with them and could benefit from their teaching and spiritual influence. Though only some of them were actually styled 'rimpoche' or 'greatly precious one', they were all alike my precious teachers and I remain deeply indebted to them and hope that in this account I have been able to give the reader at least a glimpse of them. I am grateful to Shubhra and his team at Windhorse for overseeing the production of this book, to Shantavira for his meticulous copy-editing, for a number of helpful suggestions, and for compiling the index, and to Dhammarati who, despite his many responsibilities, found time to design the cover. Above all, I am grateful to Nityabandhu, to whom, in the course of many evenings, I dictated this work and without whose co-operation it would not have seen the light.

Sangharakshita
Madhyamaloka
Birmingham
26 March 2007

As the gods worship Indra, so should one
Worship the man from whom one learns the Dharma

The Buddha
(Sutta-Nipata v.316)

Chapter One

A RED-ROBED VISITOR

I ARRIVED IN KALIMPONG IN 1950. With me was the Venerable Jagdish Kashyap, the learned Buddhist monk with whom I had been studying Pali, Abhidhamma, and Logic at Buddha Kuti, his cottage on the campus of the Benares Hindu University, where he was professor of Pali and Buddhist Philosophy. He had been professor there for twelve years and in January, when I had been with him for seven months, he decided he needed a change of scene. We would both have a holiday, he declared. He would show me some of the holy places of his native Bihar, and from there, perhaps, we would go up into the foothills of the eastern Himalayas, to a place called Kalimpong.

Spring had already come to the plains of Bihar. The sky was a tender blue, the air soft, and where the early crops were coming up the sunlit earth was a chequerboard of different shades of green. Beginning our pilgrimage at Patna, the ancient Pataliputra, Kashyap-ji and I travelled via Bihar Sharif to the very extensive ruins of the great monastic university of Nalanda, where ten thousand monks had once studied, and thence to Rajgir, where the Buddha had often lived and taught. From Rajgir we visited several places of Buddhist interest in the vicinity, the most important of them being the Vulture Peak, on which, according to Mahayana tradition, the Buddha had revealed the *White Lotus Sutra*. We spent about a month in Bihar. In the course of our travels we lectured at a college, addressed public meetings, went for alms in the traditional manner, met an eccentric American follower of a Hindu sect, and were more than once accosted by young men who, on learning that we were Buddhist monks, begged us to build a temple and propagate the Buddha's teaching. It was not until March that we reached Kalimpong, which turned out to be a pleasant hill station with a 'Norman' church, neat European-style bungalows, a colourful bazaar, and splendid views of the snows of Mount Kanchenjunga.

We were accommodated in a building belonging to the town's Newar Buddhist community, one of whose members, a young trader, Kashyap-ji had once met in Calcutta. Soon we had established a daily routine. After I had had my Pali lesson we walked through the High Street to the same trader's office, where we had lunch, on our way there passing Nepalese, Tibetans, Bhutanese, and Indians in their distinctive national or regional costumes. In the evening we received visitors, of which there were at least two or three every day. But Kashyap-ji was still restless. We had not been three weeks in Kalimpong when he informed me that he would not be returning to the Benares Hindu University. Instead, he would spend some time meditating in the jungles of Bihar, where a yogi whom he knew had a hermitage. Perhaps, as he meditated, it would become clear to him what he ought to do next. I was to remain in Kalimpong.

'Stay here and work for the good of Buddhism,' he told me as he left the following morning. 'The Newars will look after you.'

I was twenty-four, and though I had been a Buddhist for seven or eight years I did not feel experienced enough to work for the good of Buddhism, especially as I was not yet fully ordained. I also doubted whether our trader friend and his fellow Buddhist Newars were quite so ready to look after me as Kashyap-ji supposed. But the word of the guru was not to be disobeyed, and I bowed in silent acquiescence.

Though I did not know it at the time, I was to spend fourteen years in Kalimpong.

In *Facing Mount Kanchenjunga* and *In the Sign of the Golden Wheel* I have told the story of my first seven years in the town, in which I soon became a well-known figure. During those seven years I started a Young Men's Buddhist Association, edited two monthly Buddhist journals (one of them short-lived), organized Buddhist events, made many friends (and one or two enemies), studied and meditated, and wrote *A Survey of Buddhism*. I also produced a good deal of poetry, much of it inspired by the scenery in the midst of which I was living, as well as by the lives of the local people. On the whole it was a happy time. I was happy in my friendships, happy in my literary activity, and happy in my work for the good of Buddhism.

But though much was achieved, I also had to face many difficulties. My biggest difficulty was that I had no permanent base, so that I was obliged to function from a succession of borrowed or rented premises. In March 1957, exactly seven years after my arrival in Kalimpong, I was living at Everton Villa, a roomy bungalow situated in a quiet spot about a mile and a half from the bazaar. I had taken it on a year's lease, and the lease was due to expire in six months' time. Before that, I would have to find somewhere else to stay. This would not be easy, since owing to the influx of wealthy Tibetan refugees into the town it had become more and more difficult to find a house or bungalow that was to let. It was at this point that I received a visit from a celebrated Nyingma lama whom I had met a few days previously, and with whom I had already formed a strong spiritual connection. On learning that my aim was to establish in Kalimpong a permanent monastic centre dedicated to the study, practice, and dissemination of the total Buddhist tradition, but that there seemed to be little likelihood of my being able to do so, my red-robed visitor assured me, in the most emphatic manner, that I would undoubtedly establish such a centre in Kalimpong. I would establish it quite soon, and I should call it 'The Vihara Where the Three Yanas Flourish'.

Less than six weeks later, when I was in Calcutta in connection with my editorial work, I received a batch of redirected mail. Among the letters was one from the landlord of Everton Villa. Though my lease did not expire until September, he wrote requiring me to move out by 15 May, as the property had been bought by a Tibetan who insisted on immediate occupation as one of the conditions of the sale. The next letter I opened was from Marco Pallis, of whom I had seen a good deal when he was in Kalimpong in the early 1950s, and who was one of the friends to whom I had written for help. In it he promised very substantial assistance towards the realization of my plans. The result was that I was in a position to buy a small property situated on the southern outskirts of the town, about two miles from the bazaar, and on 23 May, with the help of friends who were staying with me, I moved in. The property comprised a stone cottage sheltered on the north and south by magnificent Kashmir cypresses, and four acres of terraced hillside that included a bamboo grove and a hundred orange trees. The cottage, which was perched on a rocky spur, faced due west, and commanded a panoramic view of the foothills on both the Darjeeling and Sikkim sides of the River Rangit.

The Triyana Vardhana Vihara, as I called it (this being the Sanskrit equivalent of the Tibetan name it had been given before it even existed), was to be my base for the next seven years – indeed, for the rest of my time in India.

The celebrated Nyingma lama who had predicted its establishment was Chattrul Sangye Dorje. I had met him through my Sikkimese friend Sonam Topgay Kazi, who was a great admirer of the lama and had come from Gangtok to see him and pay his respects. 'Chattrul' meant 'without affairs' or 'without concerns', Sonam Topgay explained, and he was commonly known as *Chattrul* Sangye Dorje on account of his complete indifference to such things as organized monasticism and ecclesiastical position. It was not even clear whether he was a monk or a layman. He roamed freely from place to place, no one knowing where he was going to turn up next or how long he would stay. He was an accomplished yogi, having spent many years in the solitudes of eastern Tibet, meditating; and if popular reports were to be believed he possessed many psychic powers and was a great magician. Despite his indifference to organized monasticism and ecclesiastical position, Sonam Topgay added, and his frequently bizarre and eccentric behaviour, Chattrul Sangye Dorje was highly esteemed by several prominent members of the Gelug hierarchy. Once, when in Lhasa, he had bestowed a number of esoteric Tantric initiations on the Regent of Tibet. At the conclusion of the ceremonies, which lasted several days, the Regent made the customary offerings which, his position being what it was, were extremely valuable. Chattrul Sangye Dorje swept them all onto a cloth, tied the cloth up into a bundle, and handed the bundle to the Regent, saying, 'Look after these for me.' Whereupon he resumed his wanderings.

Sonam Topgay's account intrigued me. In fact, I was fascinated by his picture of the unconventional lama who, as I later discovered, was widely revered as one of the three great Nyingma gurus of the century, the two others being Jamyang Khyentse Rimpoche and Dudjom Rimpoche. Seeing my interest, Sonam Topgay observed that it would not be difficult for me to meet the lama, who notoriously did not stand on ceremony and who was very accessible – once you had succeeded in tracking him down. He moreover hinted that although Chattrul Sangye Dorje was highly unpredictable, and one could never be sure how he would respond to a particular request, he *might* be willing to give me Tantric initiation. In any case, I ought not to miss the opportunity of meeting so great a lama and obtaining his blessing.

Thus it was that, on the morning of 8 March, I found myself in the presence of Chattrul Rimpoche, as he was also called, who was staying at Tirpai, a village on the other side of the town, on the way up to Dailo Hill. I do not know what I had expected the celebrated Nyingma lama to look like. But in any case I received something like a shock when we met. He was of indeterminate age, perhaps somewhere between thirty-five and forty-five or even fifty, his coarse black hair was cut short like a monk's, and he was clad in a nondescript maroon garment lined with what appeared to be grubby sheepskin. What I was most struck by, however, was his face, which was coarse and unrefined almost to the point of brutality, and could easily have passed for that of a horny-handed peasant with no thought beyond his pigs and poultry. At the same time, his whole being communicated such an impression of rock-like strength and reliability that one could not but feel reassured, and with Sonam Topgay as interpreter it was not long before the two of us were deep in discussion.

As was proper, Chattrul Rimpoche took the lead, and asked me a number of questions, first about the Vinaya or Code of Monastic Discipline, then about the Abhidharma. I must have answered the questions to his satisfaction, for from the Abhidharma we progressed – through what intermediate steps I no longer recollect – to meditation and meditational experience, so that I was able to tell him about the Bombay friend who received, in a state of trance, teachings and directives which he believed came from God. To what extent did he think these could be accepted? Chattrul Rimpoche's reply was in agreement with the conclusion at which I had already arrived. Teachings and directives received in a state of trance, whether by oneself or by another person, were not to be accepted uncritically but were to be subjected to the test of reason and experience and compared with the Buddhavachana, or Word of the Buddha, as explained by the Enlightened masters of India and Tibet.

By this time, I had developed considerable confidence in the Rimpoche, and I therefore asked him to tell me who my yidam or tutelary deity was. Far from showing surprise at my request, he seemed quite pleased, and after a moment of inner recollection told me that my yidam was Dolma Jungo, or Green Tara, the 'female' Bodhisattva of fearlessness and spontaneous helpfulness, adding that Tara had been the tutelary deity of many of the great pandits of India and Tibet. He then proceeded to bestow on me the appropriate initiation, first giving me the ten-syllable mantra, which he pronounced very forcefully, after which he explained the *sadhana* or spiritual practice which would enable me to identify myself with Green Tara and call down the blessing of the Bodhisattvas on myself and on all sentient beings. The latter he did at some length, so that it was mid-afternoon when I finally bade Chattrul Rimpoche a grateful farewell, having spent four hours in his company. My mood was one of considerable elation.

A few days later, Chattrul Sangye Dorje came to see me at Everton Villa. Though he probably arrived unannounced, he must have been accompanied by Sonam Topgay or another interpreter, for he explained the Green Tara sadhana to me again and gave me further instructions about its practice. I had already committed his previous explanations to writing and therefore was able to check what I had written and make sure I had got the details of the sadhana absolutely right. It was in the course of this visit that Chattrul Rimpoche, having elicited from me the information that Everton Villa was only a rented property, assured me that I would soon be able to establish the permanent monastic centre of my dreams and that I should call it 'The Vihara Where the Three Yanas Flourish'. He then addressed to me, in what was evidently a mood of high inspiration, the Tibetan originals of the following stanzas.

In the sky devoid of limits, the teaching of the Muni is
The sun, spreading the thousand rays of the three *sikshas*
  [i.e. morality, meditation, and wisdom];

Continually shining in the radiance of the impartial disciples,
May this Jambudvipa region of the Triyana be fair!

In accordance with his request, [made] in the Fire-Monkey Year
On the ninth day of the first month by the Maha Sthavira
    Sangharakshita,
This was written by the Shakya-upasaka, the Vidyadhara
Bodhivajra: [may there be] happiness and blessings!

That the stanzas were couched in the form of a response to a request probably was no more than a Tibetan literary convention, even as his styling me Mahasthavira or 'Great Elder' when I was a simple bhikshu was just the normal Tibetan politeness. That Chattrul Rimpoche should have referred to himself as the 'Shakya-upasaka' meant that technically speaking he was not a monk but a layman. Later I learned that he was not a *tulku* or 'incarnate lama', which made the esteem in which he was held by many who were tulkus all the more remarkable.

There was a reason for my asking Chattrul Sangye Dorje to tell me who my yidam or tutelary deity was. For at least seven or eight years I had been greatly preoccupied with the problem of what I called 'getting beyond the ego' (not that there really was an ego, or any question of literally getting beyond it). In fact, I had written an essay entitled 'Getting Beyond the Ego', in which I declared Buddhism to be 'satisfied with nothing less than the absolute renunciation of the ego-sense in its subtlest no less than in its grossest formulations'. One way of getting beyond, or renouncing, the ego, at least to an extent, consisted in preferring the will of another to one's own, especially the will of one's teacher or guru. Inspired by a passage in Thomas Merton's *Seeds of Contemplation*, according to which the disciple should surrender his will absolutely to the will of his spiritual superior, I resolved to apply the idea to my relations with Kashyap-ji. This I did from the time I read Merton's book, which was during our pilgrimage to the holy places of Bihar, to the time my teacher left Kalimpong for the plains, and it was because I was still applying the idea to my relations with him that I was able to obey his injunction to stay in Kalimpong and work for the good of Buddhism. Had I not obeyed it, I most likely would never have met Chattrul Rimpoche or any other great lamas who, after the Chinese occupation of Tibet, started arriving in the town as refugees.

One could also get beyond the ego by opening oneself to the transforming influence of one or other of the transcendental beings who according to the Buddhism of Tibet (and of that of China and Japan) were the different infinitely various aspects of the Buddha's Dharmakaya or Body of Truth. That Green Tara, the 'female' Bodhisattva of fearlessness and spontaneous helpfulness, was my tutelary deity meant that she was a transcendental counterpart of my own mundane nature. In other words, I had an *affinity* with Green Tara, and it was on account of that affinity that I could, by devotion to her – by *becoming* her – most readily gain access to the transcendental realm to which she belonged.

Chattrul Rimpoche did not stay long in Kalimpong. Shortly after visiting me at Everton Villa he resumed his wanderings, and we next met when both of us happened to be in Darjeeling. By that time he had picked up some Nepali, of which I also had a little knowledge, so that we had no need of an interpreter. At least, I have no recollection of anyone else being present. At one point he opened his hand to reveal a little heap of what seemed to be seed pearls. They were holy relics, he told me. When he was in Nepal he had thrust his hand inside an ancient, ruined stupa and this was what he had found. For the rest of the time I was with him he spoke in a strange, enigmatic manner that I did not find easy to follow, and the bizarre, magician-like side of his character was much more in evidence than it had been at our previous meetings.

Chapter Two

THE FRENCH NUN –
AND THE DAKINI

TIBETAN FRIENDS who came to know that the Triyana Vardhana Vihara had been given its name by Chattrul Sangye Dorje were greatly impressed. Whatever the Rimpoche blessed was sure to prosper, they told me. One of these friends was Kachu Rimpoche, the abbot of Pemayangtse Gompa, the premier Nyingma monastery of Sikkim. I first heard about Kachu Rimpoche from the turbulent and demanding Thupten Chhokyi (formerly Dominique Delannoy), known throughout the area as 'the French Nun' or, to those who knew her personally, as 'Ani-la'. Recently she had returned from a visit to Sikkim in a state of great excitement. She had found a new guru, she told me. He was a most remarkable man, and she had met him in the strangest manner.

Little by little the story of the meeting came out, Ani-la's words tumbling over one another in her eagerness to tell me everything at once. She had been wandering in the mountains of western Sikkim on her own, in a state of deep depression, thinking that life was not worth living and that the only course left to her was to commit suicide. Thus wandering, not caring in which direction she went, she came upon a small clearing in the forest. A tent had been pitched in the clearing, and in front of the tent sat a shaven-headed figure, whom she at once recognized as a lama. Her curiosity aroused, she approached and saluted him in her best Tibetan, and the two got into conversation. The lama, it transpired, was from Tibet. He was on his way to Pemayangtse Gompa, where he was to be installed as abbot. According to tradition, he had to enter the monastery on a certain auspicious day. That day had not yet come, and in the meantime he was staying on his own in the forest and meditating.

Having satisfied the French Nun's curiosity, the lama naturally expected her to satisfy his, a white woman in monastic garb no doubt being the last person he had expected to meet in the forest-clad mountains of western Sikkim. She was a *getsulma* or novice nun, Ani-la explained. Who had ordained her? Dhardo Rimpoche, a Gelug incarnate lama who lived in Kalimpong. What sadhana or spiritual practice was she doing? She was doing the sadhana of Manjughosha, 'He of the Gentle Voice', the Bodhisattva of wisdom. So far the interrogation had proceeded along familiar lines, but at this point the strange lama's expression changed.

'No,' he said, in a stern but kindly manner, 'you are *not* doing the Manjughosha sadhana. You have not done it for six months.'

Ani-la was overwhelmed. It was true. Being angry with Dhardo Rimpoche she had stopped doing the sadhana he had given her at the time of her ordination. The lama must have read her thoughts. He was a real lama. She would become his disciple. The upshot was that Ani-la spent some time at Pemayangtse Gompa after the lama's installation, and there received teachings from him.

Not long after my hearing the excited Frenchwoman's account of how she had met her new guru, Kachu Rimpoche paid a short visit to Kalimpong and I was able to meet him myself. Unfortunately I remember nothing of that first meeting. I do, however, have a vivid recollection of my second meeting with him, as well as of the way it came about. At that time I was on friendly terms with an American couple, Simmons and Marcia Roof, who happened to be spending the hot season in the cooler atmosphere of Kalimpong. Simmons was a Unitarian minister who was in India on a study sabbatical. He was collecting material for a book on the spiritual life, as illustrated by his personal religious quest, and in this connection he was anxious to meet as many spiritual personalities as possible. When I told Simmons Ani-la's story, adding that the lama was just then paying a second visit to Kalimpong, he and Marcia begged me to arrange a meeting. I therefore invited Kachu Rimpoche to lunch, with the result that a day or two later my two American friends found themselves face to face with their first Tibetan lama.

Kachu Rimpoche must have been about forty at the time. Cheerful, straightforward, and down-to-earth, he certainly did not give the impression of being possessed of supernormal powers of any kind. There was no doubt that he was very knowledgeable, however, and over lunch, and for some time afterwards, Simmons plied him with questions on a wide variety of topics, with me acting as interpreter and translating his questions from English into Nepali and Kachu Rimpoche's answers from Nepali into English. As the discussion progressed, the questions Simmons asked related to topics of a more and more abstruse nature. All the Rimpoche's answers, as well as his additional explanations, were clear and to the point, especially when the questions related to meditation, of which he evidently had extensive personal experience. At times, the alternation of question and answer was so rapid I had difficulty keeping up with my translations. Eventually, when Simmons had put a highly philosophical question regarding the nature of Nirvana, I noticed that the Rimpoche had started replying to it without waiting for me to translate it for him. He was replying not to the words of the question, which was in a language he did not understand, but to the thoughts (and possibly also to the feelings) behind the question, which it seemed he was able to comprehend directly without having to rely on its verbal expression. For some reason, Simmons failed to notice this, but after Kachu Rimpoche's departure he and Marcia expressed themselves entirely satisfied with the meeting, which had exceeded their expectations.

According to Buddhist tradition, *parachittajnana*, knowledge of the minds of others, was one of the mundane *abhijnas* or super-knowledges. Though a sign of attainment in meditation, its development was not essential to the attainment of Enlightenment. That Kachu Rimpoche was able to know Simmons' mind, if such indeed had been the case, did not in itself mean that he was far advanced spiritually. Nonetheless, that day's meeting left me deeply impressed by him and anxious to continue the acquaintance, despite the fact that he was living in western Sikkim and I in Kalimpong. As it happened, he was of much the same mind, with the result that in subsequent years we met a number of times and he came to occupy an important place in my life as friend and teacher.

I wish I could say he came to occupy a similar place in the life of the French Nun. Unfortunately, she soon became no less dissatisfied with him than she had been with Dhardo Rimpoche, even though she was permitted to stay again at Pemayangtse Gompa and received more teachings. One of her bitterest complaints, to which I had to listen more than once, was that the Rimpoche spent far too much time talking with his brother, who was also a monk and lived at the monastery and was, according to the exigent Frenchwoman, a thoroughly bad influence on her guru. As I knew only too well, Ani-la regarded time spent talking to others which could have been spent talking with *her* as time wasted. Another complaint was that at Pemayangtse alcohol was employed in the monastery's ritual, this being in accordance with Nyingma tradition. Once, when Kachu Rimpoche was sprinkling the images of the Buddhas and Bodhisattvas with a few drops of whisky, she had, by her own admission, protested against the desecration (as she considered it to be) in a way that was highly disrespectful both to the Nyingma tradition and to her guru. It was not surprising, therefore, that not many months after her unexpected meeting with Kachu Rimpoche she should have found herself not only again without a guru but pouring out her troubles to Jamyang Khyentse Rimpoche, who had recently arrived in the district and was staying in Darjeeling. For this she was gently rebuked by Princess Pema Tsedeun of Sikkim. The Rimpoche had his own worries, the princess told her (he was unwell at the time) and she should not bother him.

By this time I had met the great Nyingma guru myself. I met him not in Darjeeling but in Kalimpong, at Panorama, the guest cottage where I had lived for six months in 1951 as the guest of Prince K.M. Latthakin, the nephew and son-in-law of the last king of Burma. My first impression of Jamyang Khyentse Rimpoche was that he was very much a *monk*. With his closely cropped white hair, long earlobes, and deeply lined face, he indeed looked more like a Burmese *mahathera* or 'great elder' than a Tibetan incarnate lama. On my entering the room with Sonam Topgay he looked up from his book and asked me, when I had been introduced, 'Do you know anything about dancing?' I was obliged to admit that I was completely ignorant of the subject. Slightly disappointed, the old man explained to Sonam Topgay, and Sonam Topgay explained to me, that he had been reading about dancing, there being a dozen or so works on dance in the *Tenjur*, the voluminous collection of non-canonical texts of various kinds. The works on dance, all translated from Sanskrit, were the choreographic basis of the Tibetan so-called 'lama dances', and this was why the Rimpoche was studying them. As well as being an accomplished yogi, he was a polymath who had taken all Tibetan knowledge for his province and was ready, moreover, to acquire information even from a casual Western visitor.

The next time Kachu Rimpoche was in Kalimpong I was therefore able to tell him that I had met Jamyang Khyentse Rimpoche. He was delighted to hear this, for he had a boundless admiration for the celebrated old lama, whom he regarded as his guru. But it was not enough, he told me bluntly, to meet a great guru like Jamyang Khyentse Rimpoche. I should ask for a *wangkur* (literally 'empowerment') or Tantric initiation, and since the Rimpoche, as his name indicated, was regarded as a manifestation of Jamyang or Manjughosha, the Bodhisattva of wisdom, it was for initiation into the following of that Bodhisattva that I should ask. Kachu Rimpoche spoke so earnestly, and was so evidently desirous of my spiritual welfare, that I could not but heed his advice. Nonetheless, I did not want to be like those Tibetan Buddhists who collected wangkurs in much the same way as English schoolboys collected postage stamps, rare specimens being especially prized by both sorts of collectors. Wangkurs were empowerments to *practise* a sadhana, and I had to be sure I wanted to take on another sadhana, in addition to the one I had received from Chattrul Rimpoche. Eventually I decided I did want to, and that I ought to approach Jamyang Khyentse Rimpoche without further delay.

In the third week of October 1957 I therefore left for Darjeeling, where the great Nyingma guru was then staying. Kachu Rimpoche was also staying there, though not with Khyentse Rimpoche but with a Tibetan family in the bazaar, and in the afternoon I went to see my warm-hearted lama friend. We talked for a while, after which I sat while he performed a Lakshmi puja, it being the birthday of Tsering Chodron, Khyentse Rimpoche's *dakini* or spiritual consort. I was familiar with Lakshmi as a popular Hindu goddess, the granter of wealth and prosperity, and I was therefore not a little surprised to find a Tibetan incarnate lama performing a lengthy puja in her honour. I subsequently discovered that the four-armed goddess had been absorbed into the Buddhist pantheon, and that under the name of Shri she featured in the *Suvarnaprabhasa Sutra* or 'Sutra of Golden Light', a Mahayana scripture on which I was to give a series of lectures many years later. The following morning, having spent the night at the house of a Bengali doctor I knew, I called on Kachu Rimpoche at his lodging and together we made our way to Cooch Behar House, which the Maharaja of Cooch Behar had placed at Khyentse Rimpoche's disposal. After we had talked with the Maharani of Sikkim, who was also staying there, we were ushered into the presence of the great guru, who received us with his usual kindness and dignity of manner. Kachu Rimpoche spoke for me, as I think had been arranged between us beforehand. The English monk wished to ask the venerable master for a wangkur, he said, speaking in the flowery Tibetan appropriate to the occasion. Would the venerable master please grant his request. Khyentse Rimpoche's expression showed that the request had pleased him. He would give me not one wangkur but three or four, he told me. I should come back on Thursday, as he would have to get the books he needed for the ceremony from Gangtok. It was then Saturday.

On Wednesday night I slept badly, though not because I was excited at the prospect of receiving initiation from Khyentse Rimpoche but because for the last two days I had been suffering from an extremely painful swelling of the gums. Nonetheless, I had travelled up to Darjeeling that afternoon so as to be quite sure I was not late for the ceremony the following day. I was still in considerable pain when on the morning of 24 October Kachu Rimpoche and I made our way to Cooch Behar House for the second time that week, and the right side of my face was badly swollen.

The initiation was an intimate affair, with Khyentse Rimpoche presiding grandfather-like over his spiritual family. He sat cross-legged on a kind of throne made up of three or four big, square Tibetan cushions placed one on top of another; in front of him was a narrow table on which were arranged a dorje and bell, a pot with a long, curved spout, a small pot filled with rice, and other ritual implements. On the guru's left, on a single cushion, sat 'the Dakini', as she was respectfully called, and on *her* left, also on a single cushion, sat the Maharani of Sikkim. On the right of the guru were his personal attendant, another monk, Kachu Rimpoche, and my good Dharma-friend Sonam Topgay Kazi. My place was immediately in front of the Rimpoche. (I was later told that in the Hinayana one kept one's eyes respectfully lowered in the presence of one's teacher, but that in the Vajrayana one looked the guru in the face.) Partly because the proceedings were in Tibetan (though Sonam Topgay translated whatever I was required to repeat after Khyentse Rimpoche), and partly because I was in pain, I remembered little of the elaborate ceremony, which lasted from 10.00 a.m. to 2.00 p.m. I did, however, remember offering Jamyang Khyentse a mandala or symbolic representation of the universe, and noticing with what reverence his attendant monk offered him the pointed red pandit hat which he donned at certain key points in the ceremony. Above all, I remember the rapt, beatific expression with which he looked up as he invoked the Bodhisattvas whose wangkurs he was conferring upon me. It was as if he actually saw their diaphanous, rainbow-like forms floating in the air before him. Whether or not it was the Manjughosha initiation which Kachu Rimpoche had asked Jamyang Khyentse to give me I do not know, but Manjughosha was invoked first, then Avalokiteshvara, next Vajrapani, and finally Tara, so that by the time the last tinkle of Khyentse Rimpoche's ritual bell had died away I had been empowered to practise the sadhanas of all four Bodhisattvas.

In order to practise the sadhanas I would need to have the texts describing them, and these the Maharani undertook to provide. She would have copies made when she returned to Gangtok, she said, and would send them to me. They arrived a few weeks later. Naturally they were in Tibetan, which I did not understand, least of all the classical Tibetan in which the texts were composed. Luckily I had a friend who did understand it and who, moreover, was willing to translate my texts for me. The friend was John Driver, an English scholar of about my own age who was doing research into the Nyingma tantras for a doctoral thesis. Dreamy and absent-minded (or at least appearing so), he lived with his wife Anne and their two – later three – daughters in a house within the Scottish Mission compound called the White House, but which, for the purposes of our correspondence, we renamed the White Tara House. It did not take John long to translate the sadhanas of Manjughosha and Avalokiteshvara, but for reasons I no longer recollect he never got round to translating those of Vajrapani and Tara, even though he made for me English versions of several other Tibetan Buddhist texts.

I had now received altogether five tantric initiations, one from Chattrul Rimpoche and four from Jamyang Khyentse Rimpoche. For the last eight months I had been practising the Green Tara sadhana given me by the former, and to this I now added the practice of the Manjughosha-stuti sadhana. I practised them early each morning, in the order in which I had received them, after chanting the traditional Pali verses in praise of the Buddha, the Dharma, and the Sangha. Later on, I came to see the two sadhanas as being not mutually exclusive but complementary, inasmuch as Green Tara and Manjughosha, like Avalokiteshvara, Vajrapani, Ksitigarbha, and the rest, were aspects or emanations of the Buddha's Dharmakaya or Body of Truth. The fact that I was now practising tantric meditation did not, however, mean the complete abandonment of *anapana-sati* or respiration-mindfulness, which had been the sheet anchor of my spiritual life for nine years or more. Though I did not practise it regularly, as I had previously done, I had recourse to it, as to an old and tried friend, whenever I found it necessary to calm and concentrate my mind before proceeding to sadhana practice. Mindfulness in the broader sense I continued to cultivate assiduously, doing my best to remain aware of whatever I thought, said, did, and felt throughout the day.

Three weeks after receiving the four wangkurs from Khyentse Rimpoche I saw him again, this time in Kalimpong. He was staying at Arunachal, the Kalimpong home of Princess Pema Tsedeun and her Tibetan husband Pheunkhang-sey, who like his two incarnate lama brothers was well known to me. Arunachal was situated not far from the Vihara, and from its position high above the road commanded an even finer view. I found Khyentse Rimpoche walking stiffly in the garden, enjoying the warmth of the late autumn sunshine. The Dakini was with him, as was Kachu Rimpoche, who was staying with me at the time and had preceded me. As I very much wanted to have a photograph of my guru I had arranged for a professional photographer to be present and Rimpoche agreed to sit for him. He sat in an armchair in the garden, upright and dignified, his hands resting on his knees, and gently smiling. At my request the Dakini, too, agreed to sit for her photograph. I gathered that this was

a great favour, as normally she did not allow herself to be photo-
graphed. But in view of her close spiritual relationship with Khyentse Rimpoche, I was keen to have a photograph of her as well, and
perhaps she had understood this.

Kachu Rimpoche had been at pains to assure me that the relationship between Khyentse Rimpoche and the beautiful young woman
was not a sexual one, though the thought that it might be of such a
nature had not so much as crossed my mind. No one who had seen
them together could imagine the relationship to be other than a spiritual one. Some years ago, so Kachu Rimpoche told me, an astrologer
had predicted that the Rimpoche would die at the age of fifty-seven.
Other senior lamas, as well as his own disciples, had therefore
begged him to 'take' a dakini or spiritual consort, since according to
tantric tradition the taking of a dakini could prolong a lama's life,
thereby enabling him to continue benefiting humanity by teaching
the Dharma. Fortunately, a dakini was at hand, in the person of the
daughter of Khyentse Rimpoche's secretary, and a year or two ago
he had 'married' her.

Now I could understand that a sexual relationship with a dakini
might well have a rejuvenating effect on an elderly lama, and even,
perhaps, prolong his life. Such a relationship would be marriage in
the ordinary sense of the term, and the 'dakini' would simply be the
lama's wife. But how could a purely spiritual relationship with a
dakini have the effect of prolonging the life of the lama who took her
as his consort? For the members of Khyentse Rimpoche's spiritual
family, his consort was not only 'the Dakini'; she was also his chief
disciple and a spiritual personality in her own right. She was ever
calm and serene, never seeking to draw attention to herself or putting herself forward. Above all, she was deeply devoted to Khyentse
Rimpoche. Her devotion was not of the emotional, quasi-erotic kind
that some female disciples direct towards their guru. I cannot
remember seeing her actually looking at the Rimpoche, or, for that
matter, him looking at her, in a way that suggested there was something special between them. It was as though she felt his presence in
her heart and that was enough. Was it, then, the strength and purity
of her devotion that was prolonging Jamyang Khyentse's life, if
indeed that was what was happening? But Kachu Rimpoche and the
other disciples were also deeply devoted to him. Could not their

devotion have the same kind of effect, or was the Dakini's devotion qualitatively different from theirs? On the other hand, it might be that by having a purely spiritual relationship with a dakini a lama could not, in fact, prolong his life, and that although Khyentse Rimpoche ostensibly had taken a dakini for the traditional reason, his relationship with her was really of a quite different kind.

Before leaving Kalimpong, the guru paid a visit to the Triyana Vardhana Vihara. He came escorted by Kachu Rimpoche, who brought him by car, as he was not able to walk even the comparatively short distance from Arunachal to the Vihara. With him he brought the plump, 8-year-old Sogyal Rimpoche, whom I had already seen at Arunachal, who was shaven-headed like his elders and wore a junior version of their maroon robes. A throne had been prepared for Jamyang Khyentse in the shrine-room, and when he had taken his seat the dozen or more friends and students of mine whom I had invited to meet the Rimpoche and obtain his blessing offered him white ceremonial scarves or *khata*, as did I and the other inmates of the Vihara. Rimpoche then gave me, of his own accord, the *lung* or 'permission to read' a certain devotional text, after which he performed a ritual of purification and blessing for the benefit of the Vihara and those who were gathered there. I then escorted him back to Arunachal. He had spent altogether an hour with us.

My next two meetings with Khyentse Rimpoche both took place in Gangtok, which I visited from time to time and where I frequently lectured on the Dharma, sometimes at the invitation of the Maharajkumar of Sikkim and sometimes at the invitation of Apa Sahib Pant, the Government of India's Political Officer in Sikkim. Both meetings took place, moreover, at the white-walled, yellow-roofed palace *lhakhang* or temple, where the Rimpoche was then staying and where he died in 1959, aged sixty-seven. On each occasion I went simply to pay my respects, and each time I received a gift from him. The first gift was a *thangka* or painted scroll, resplendent with the traditional border of rich Chinese brocade and mounted on rollers. The big central figure was that of a saffron-coloured Manjughosha, who with his right hand whirled aloft a flaming sword of insight while with his left he grasped the stem of a white lotus flower on whose open petals rested a sacred book, understood to be that of the Perfection of Wisdom. He was flanked on his right by a white, four-armed Avalokiteshvara, and on his left by a dark blue Vajrapani in his wrathful form. Below Manjughosha was Green Tara, and above him, in three tiers, a couple of dozen human teachers of whom I recognized only the Buddha and Milarepa. Two wrathful deities, one blue and one red, occupied, respectively, the left-hand and right-hand bottom corners of the painting, while to the right of the book of the Perfection of Wisdom there was a range of snow-covered mountains. In two of the mountains there was a cave, and in each cave sat a tiny yellow-robed figure.

The painting was not so well executed as he could have wished, Jamyang Khyentse told me, though it was the work of the best artist he had been able to find in Gangtok; and indeed, the work was clumsily if painstakingly done, the rays of rainbow light that emanated from Manjughosha's body terminating in a ring of solid-looking rainbow balls. But I was too deeply moved by the Rimpoche's kindness in giving me the thangka, which had been painted in accordance with his directions, to be much concerned about any shortcomings it might have. Moreover, there was a special significance in his giving me the thangka. As he proceeded to explain, through the initiations he had given me he had transmitted to me the essence of the teachings of the great masters who were depicted in it. I was now their spiritual heir and successor. Smiling, he then pointed to the yellow-robed figures in their caves, one meditating and one teaching. Both were me.

The second gift I received from Khyentse Rimpoche was one he may not have been aware he was giving, though in my eyes this did not render it any the less a gift. On my arrival at the palace temple that day I was asked to wait, as the Rimpoche was engaged. I must have waited for half an hour or more, and when he eventually emerged from an inner room, he apologized for having kept me waiting. A lama who was an old friend of his had just died, he explained, and he had been reciting the Vajrasattva mantra for his benefit. Reciting the Vajrasattva mantra! The words took an immediate hold on me. It was as though Khyentse Rimpoche was giving me a teaching. The teaching was to the effect that the Vajrasattva mantra should be recited for the benefit of the dead. Thereafter, following my guru's example, I recited it whenever I heard that someone connected with me had died.

Chapter Three

A DAMSEL IN DISTRESS

TOWARDS THE END OF 1957 I received a letter superscribed 'In Confidence'. It was from Ronald Boughen, a courier at the UK High Commission in New Delhi. We had met in the Indian capital, and he had visited Kalimpong. A large, sandy-haired man of about forty, he was a Buddhist of the devotional rather than the intellectual type, and though we were not exactly friends he wrote to me frequently, sometimes at considerable length, and often on official notepaper. He usually wrote about his personal problems, especially those that tended to arise in connection with his relationships with various youthful protégés. This time, however, he wrote to inform me that Mme Marie-Elise Langford-Rae had told him that she would be in Kalimpong later that month. She was married to the Kazi Dorje of Chakhung, who had come to Delhi to see the President, and who was involved, so he understood, in the Sikkim-Tibet trade. Mme Langford-Rae, or the Kazini Sahiba of Chakhung, as she now called herself, was very worried about her stay in Kalimpong, for she felt someone might cause her some trouble.

'I do not know on what grounds she bases her fears,' Ronald wrote. 'However, if anything does go amiss I should be grateful if you would keep me in the picture.'

The person who was the subject of this rather mysterious letter was not unfamiliar to me, at least by sight. A blonde, smiling woman in her forties, she had been in Kalimpong in 1950, staying at the Himalayan Hotel, and I had more than once seen her driving around with Mr Lha Tsering, the much-feared boss of the Kalimpong branch of the Central Intelligence Bureau, who was a staunch supporter of mine. The Kazi Sahib I had met once, in Darjeeling, and I remembered him as a 50-year-old man who wore Western dress and spoke very little English. How had the former Mrs Langford-Rae come to marry him, and why, if she was coming to join him in his Kalimpong home, should she be so worried about her stay in the town? I was soon to find out.

A few days after the arrival of Ronald's letter I received a note from the Kazini Sahiba. It was written from Arcadia, a bungalow situated on the main road into Kalimpong. In it she begged me to come and see her as soon as I conveniently could as she was badly in need of help and advice. I left the Vihara almost immediately and was soon with her. She was still blonde, but she certainly was not smiling. Indeed, she tended to act the 'damsel in distress', and with her long black gown seemed almost to have dressed for the part. I quickly realized that beneath the histrionics she was genuinely worried about what Ronald had tactfully termed her 'stay in Kalimpong'. No doubt it was because she was worried about this that she had brought with her a companion in the shape of a short, fierce-looking old lady with a pure white quiff. This was her dear, dear sister – her adopted sister – Helen, the Kazini Sahiba explained, throwing her arms round the old lady, who out of loyalty and devotion had come with her all the way from Delhi and would be sharing her new life in Kalimpong.

Rather to my surprise, the Kazi Sahib was not with them, and it soon transpired that Arcadia was not his own house, as I had assumed, but a place he had rented for his new wife and her companion. His house was situated in another part of the town, and under its roof there still lived a woman whom the Kazini described as a despicable creature for whom the Kazi had once cared, and whom he was unable, or unwilling, to throw out. Apparently the Kazi had neglected to be off with the old love before he was on with the new. Or perhaps he had not considered what effect his marriage to the Kazini might have on his existing domestic arrangements. In any case, the Kazini was insistent that the other woman should be evicted forthwith and herself installed as mistress of the house, and the help and advice she wanted from me was with regard to this end. Since I did not really know the Kazi, having met him only once, I did not feel able to intervene in connection with so personal a matter. I therefore confined myself, then and subsequently, to counselling patience and giving the Kazini what moral support I could in her predicament, the humiliating nature of which she felt keenly. How long she and Helen had to stay at Arcadia I do not remember, but eventually the day came when, escorted by the Kazi and me, the Kazini and her companion were driven to their new home, smuggled in through the front door, and hurried into two rooms at the rear of the building. The Kazini had achieved one, at least, of her objectives, but only one, and it was hardly a glorious victory. The other woman still occupied the front bedroom of the bungalow.

In the course of the next few days I came to understand the situation better, though I never understood it completely. The Kazi had been married to the woman in the front bedroom for some thirty years. She belonged to the same aristocratic land-owning class as himself, and the marriage had been celebrated in accordance with Sikkimese customs. They had no children. She had been of no help to him in his business and political activities, and no comfort to him personally, and they had long since ceased to be effectively married. It was not surprising, therefore, that the Kazi should have seen the articulate, highly educated and well-informed Mme Langford-Rae as an ideal partner in every way and have wanted to marry her. Thus it came about that, at the start of the New Year, Kazi Lhendup Dorje, as he was generally known, had the old love and the new love under his roof at the same time. What was to be done? The present situation could not be allowed to continue. It was highly unsatisfactory, especially to the Kazini, who could not be expected to remain confined indefinitely to the two back rooms like a prisoner. In the end, tradition came to the rescue in the form of a *panchayat*.

A panchayat was a group of five persons who judged disputes and disagreements between two parties. Each of the parties would nominate two members of the panchayat and jointly nominate the chairman, usually someone of position or prestige in the community. The panchayat was an institution well known in the villages of India, and known also, as I now discovered, to the local Sikkimese and Tibetans, though I believe they did not strictly follow the Indian model. In the present instance the panchayat consisted of Lha Tsering, now retired from Government service, myself, two Tibetans, one of whom I knew slightly, and Gergen Tharchin, the genial Ladakhi Christian editor of the *Tibet Mirror* ('the only Tibetan newspaper in the world') whom I had met on a number of occasions. Lha Tsering and I had been nominated by the Kazini, though it was not clear to me in what way she was a party to the dispute, which was really between the Kazi and the woman in the front bedroom, who must have nominated either the two Tibetans or one of the Tibetans and Tharchin.

The panchayat met in the Kazi's comfortable lounge. It met daily for nearly a week, each session lasting three or four hours and involving the consumption of numerous cups of tea and, I suspect, after my departure, a very different kind of liquid refreshment. The Kazi was present throughout in his double capacity as host and as one of the parties to the dispute, *de facto* if not *de jure*. The proceedings were conducted by turns – sometimes simultaneously – in Tibetan, Hindi, Nepali, and English, so that at times in was not easy for me to follow the debate. In the course of the first two sessions I gradually realized that the separation between the Kazi and the woman in the front bedroom had already taken place, and that, Sikkimese customs being what they were, this had required little more than the consent of both parties. What the debate was really all about was money, or money and property, and what the panchayat had to decide was the amount of the compensation (if that was the right word) to be paid by the Kazi to the woman who, after all, had been his wife – in the eyes of their world – for thirty years.

This naturally involved a good deal of discussion, as the panchayat's decision had to be unanimous, and agreement was not quickly or easily arrived at. There were two interruptions to the proceedings. During one of the sessions there suddenly came from the back rooms the doleful sound of the Kazini's raised voice.

'They want to kill my Kazi,' she wailed. 'They want to kill my Kazi.'

We all froze. Who 'they' were was not apparent, nor did the Kazini afterwards explain what she meant. But the wailings were not repeated, and after a few minutes we resumed our discussions as if we had heard nothing, for the Kazini should not really have been on the premises. During another session the Kazi suddenly burst into tears.

'He still loves her!' exclaimed Tharchin, meaning the woman in the front bedroom. 'He still loves her!'

Whether because he was a warm-hearted, kindly man, or whether because, as a minister of the Gospel, he believed in the indissolubility of marriage, even marriage between heathen Buddhists, he evidently would have liked to see a reconciliation between the Kazi and his former wife. This was the last thing anybody else wanted, and Lha Tsering quickly intervened to head off any move in that direction. To me it seemed that the Kazi's tears were forced from him by long-repressed bitterness over his marriage, and relief that it was now over. Be that as it may, he soon recovered himself, and by the end of the next session the panchayat had come to a decision. The Kazi was to give his former wife twenty thousand rupees (the Vihara had cost only a little less) together with a house he owned in Darjeeling.

The panchayat's decision having been communicated to the lady, she emerged from the front bedroom, the door of which opened directly into the lounge. I had not seen her before. She was a tall, gaunt woman, and wore the traditional long Sikkimese (and Tibetan) ankle-length gown or *bokku*, which in this case happened to be dark blue. As was the custom, the Kazi immediately handed her the twenty thousand rupees in cash, whereupon she stuffed the thick bundle of currency notes into the bosom of her bokku and, accompanied by a handsome young nephew of the Kazi who had been helping her with her packing, left by jeep for Darjeeling.

The Kazini was now able to emerge from her seclusion with propriety. She emerged alone – without Helen. She and her dear sister had quarrelled, and the latter had returned in high dudgeon to Delhi, though not before the Kazi had given her a first class railway ticket. I had once had a brush with the haughty old lady myself, in connection with an argument she had got into with the Kazini. She was being unreasonable, I told her, with rather more frankness than tact.

'*Me? Unreasonable?*' she shrieked, her white quiff quivering with indignation.

The days following the former wife's departure were days of discovery. The servant discovered under the bed in the front bedroom a dozen or more empty whisky bottles, and the Kazini discovered that her predecessor had been having an affair with the handsome young nephew. What was more, she discovered that the Kazi had known about the affair all along. This both surprised and angered her, and she upbraided the Kazi for his having parted with twenty thousand rupees and a house when, the woman having committed adultery, he could have thrown her out of the house without giving her a single anna. But the Kazi was unrepentant, and refused to discuss the matter with her. He had handled the situation in the way he thought best, he seemed to be saying, and there was nothing more to be said.

My own discovery, a week or two later, was that the Kazini's original fear that someone in Kalimpong might cause her trouble was not entirely baseless. We were walking round the bungalow's garden one morning, talking, when suddenly an arrow whizzed past the Kazini's head missing her by inches. On another occasion I was with her in the back room she had made into a study for herself. She was standing near the open window. Suddenly she leapt back with a scream. A woman with a knife was crouching outside the window, ready to stab her as soon as she turned her back. Though the Kazi and the servant searched the garden they could find no trace of the woman, and I could see that the Kazi was inclined to think that the Kazini had imagined the whole thing, just as previously he had been inclined to regard the arrow as a random shot not intended for her. The Kazini, on the other hand, was convinced that on both occasions her life had been threatened and that behind the threat there lurked the vengeful figure of the discarded wife.

Owing to the nature of the circumstances under which we first met, I soon got to know the Kazi and Kazini very well, especially the Kazini, the Kazi being often away in Gangtok in connection with his business and political activities. In fact, there developed between the three of us a strong friendship. 'When shall we three meet again?' the Kazini would chant whenever I went up to Chakhung House (as she had renamed the bungalow) to say goodbye to them before leaving Kalimpong for one of my extensive preaching tours in the plains. Even in the early days of our friendship, it was obvious to me that the Sikkimese aristocrat and the European lady were very different in character and temperament, and even if theirs was not a case of opposites attracting each other there were, nonetheless, sufficient points of difference between them to ensure that the sparks would sometimes fly. The Kazini was outspoken, tended to be sweeping in her judgements, saw things in black and white, and was inclined to exaggerate and dramatize, though I never knew her be untruthful.

Moreover, she never gave anyone the chance to deceive her or let her down twice. 'If they will do it once, they will do it again,' she would say firmly. The Kazi, being both businessman and politician, did not always say what was in his mind, rarely adopted an extreme position, was patient and forbearing, and believed in giving those who had disappointed him a second and even a third chance. He was also ready to do even a political opponent a good turn if he could, which was an attitude the Kazini found difficult to understand.

I therefore was not surprised when I learned that in his younger days the Kazi had spent some time in a monastery. He had been head lama of Rumtek Gompa, which was the premier Kagyu monastery in Sikkim, just as Pemayangtse was the premier Nyingma one. He had been deprived of his position, on false charges, in order to make way for someone else. This happened to be the future Maharajkumar of Sikkim, who was not then the Maharajkumar or Crown Prince as his elder brother was still living. The injustice he had suffered continued to rankle with the Kazi, and it was one of the reasons for his hatred of the Maharajkumar – a hatred to which he rarely gave open expression – and his determination, as a politician, to see the overthrow of the Namgyal dynasty and the establishment of democracy in Sikkim. Yet despite his long immersion in politics and business, and his Western dress, he had not altogether ceased to be a lama. When at home he would often finger his *mala* or rosary, at the same time murmuring a mantra, or read to himself from a little Tibetan book. One day I asked him what the book was. It was the *Dorje Chopa,* he replied, rather to my astonishment, for the *Dorje Chopa* was the Tibetan translation of the *Vajracchedika* or 'Diamond Cutter' Sutra, also known simply as the *Diamond Sutra,* a text belonging to the Prajnaparamita or 'Perfection of Wisdom' class of Mahayana scriptures. As I well remembered, it was on my encountering the *Diamond Sutra,* some twelve or fourteen years earlier, that I had realized I was a Buddhist and had, in fact, always been one.

The Kazini knew nothing of Buddhist doctrine, but she had lived in Burma and had been deeply impressed by what she saw of the Buddhist way of life there. Now that she was married to a Buddhist, she ought, she felt, to take the religion more seriously. She ought, in fact, to study it. For the next few months, therefore, she spent much of her time reading the books I lent her. She also talked about the Dharma with her husband, but neither his English nor her Hindi was good enough for them to be able to discuss the finer points of the Buddha's teaching. For that kind of discussion she relied on me, as well as relying on me for basic instruction in meditation. It soon became evident that she was drawn more to the rational and ethical aspects of Buddhism than to its devotional and contemplative aspects. Not that this really mattered. By the time the anniversary of the Buddha's attainment of Enlightenment came round she was ready to declare herself a Buddhist, which she did at the Vihara in the traditional manner. At my suggestion, she wrote a report of the event for the Buddhist monthly journal I edited. It appeared under the heading 'Kazini Sahiba of Chakhung Initiated into Buddhism' and read, in part, as follows.

> Kazini Elisa-Maria Dorji-Khangsarpa of Chakhung took the Pancha Sila at the Triyana Vardhana Vihara in Kalimpong on the Vaisakha Purnima Day, Saturday the 3rd May, 2502, after having studied with her guru, the Venerable Sangharakshita, Bhikshu-in-Charge of the Vihara. The wife of the Kazi Sahib of Chakhung, Sikkim, Kazini Sahiba was born in Scotland, but brought up in Belgium where she was educated, later returning to Edinburgh University for advanced studies. She has studied and travelled in many parts of the world, and, on completion of her studies in Europe, she went to live in Burma, where she was first attracted to Buddhism.

> Travelling throughout the length and breadth of Burma, the Chinese frontier on one side, the Chin Hills, the Kachin Hills, the Manipur border, she was always deeply impressed by what she saw of the way of the life of Buddhists. Later, in her travels which took her to China, Malaya, Thailand, Morocco, Turkey, Egypt, and even to Iceland, she always felt influenced by what she had seen of Buddhism in Burma.

This was the nearest the Kazini ever came to telling the story of her life, parts of which were shrouded in mystery. From time to time, however, she told me things that enabled me to fill in some of the gaps. In Burma, for instance, she and her first husband had known the future author of *Animal Farm* and *Nineteen Eighty-Four*. They had known him not as George Orwell but as Eric Blair. He was then in the Burma Police, and every now and then she and Langford-Rae would find themselves handing over to him, or taking over from him, as they were posted to different towns around the country. Nor was George Orwell the only famous person she had known. She had interviewed Mussolini and had lived for two years in the palace of Kemal Ataturk, from whom she had received more than two hundred letters, all now deposited with a bank. In recent years (it was not clear for how many) she had lived in Delhi, teaching French at a school run by the Christian Brothers, and moving in diplomatic and political circles.

Several of the Kazini's Delhi friends knew me. One of these friends was Ronald Boughen of the UK High Commission. On her confiding to him that she was very worried about her forthcoming stay in Kalimpong, he had naturally written to me about her and asked me to keep him in the picture if anything went amiss. Something had indeed gone amiss, at the beginning of the Kazini's stay, and I had kept Ronald in the picture both then and subsequently. Thus the ball of our correspondence was kept rolling between us. I continued to hear about what he called his domestic problems and, eventually, about his plans to visit Kalimpong, which he did the following year. In the course of this visit he had a curious experience, about which he wrote to me after his return to Delhi. Just after his arrival in Kalimpong something had gone wrong with him, he wrote, and he had suffered a mental breakdown.

> The previous evening I had gone to see Joe Cann. He spoke to me of tantricism and mentioned that the Nepalese were not all they were meant to be. He spoke of many things and in a mysterious way; from then I hated everyone who was not Buddhist. I came back to Delhi in a state of collapse. Now I am again well, I have had to think over things and realize how awful I must have seemed.... I assure you on everything that is Holy, that I was the victim of some form of Auto Suggestion. It is not my way or my nature to be a person who hates anything.... I am however convinced that I was in a sick state from the time I left Joe Cann's place. Is it possible that something he said played on my mind? I feel that this was so, for also I became quite unwell and could not reason the thing at all.

It was not my way or my nature to be a person who hates anything. It was a *cri de cœur* and I knew it to be true. Ronald was of a kindly, generous disposition. I also knew that Joe Cann was just the opposite. Thin, irritable, impatient, and highly strung, the chain-smoking sexagenarian was an inveterate backbiter and scandalmonger and had the most venomous tongue in Kalimpong. He had arrived in the town soon after me, and for a short time was associated with me in my work for the Dharma. But his attitude towards me had always been highly ambivalent, and it was not long before I found myself the object of his barbed attacks, mainly on account of what he saw as my refusal to accept the advice and guidance of those older and wiser than myself. Where had all this bitterness and hatred come from? I concluded, eventually, that Joe Cann suffered from a chronic inferiority complex. The fact that someone was better than, or superior to, himself in some way – socially or educationally, for example – made him painfully conscious of his inferiority not only in that respect but in general. So painful was that consciousness, indeed, that he felt compelled to criticize, disparage, and denigrate the person concerned, and in this way bring them crashing to the ground. It may therefore have been some perceived superiority of Ronald's that had prompted Joe Cann's negative remarks about the Nepalese, knowing as he did that the close friend who had accompanied Ronald to Kalimpong was Nepalese and, what was more, not a Buddhist. On the other hand, Joe Cann had within him such a store of pent up bitterness and hatred that it needed no prompting to break out. Probably it was not something he said that had played on Ronald's mind, as the latter felt, so much as the intensity of the negative emotions to which he had been exposed in the course of his evening with the chain-smoking old man. As I knew from my own past experience, to listen to Joe Cann's tirades for any length of time was to be injected with a kind of psychic poison that could leave one feeling physically ill.

Shortly after his visit to Kalimpong there began to appear in Ronald's letters passing references to 'the Lady of Kulu'. As I came to know afterwards, this mysterious personage was the widow of an old friend of Ronald's, a British army officer who, after his retirement from active service, had settled in the Kulu Valley, a particularly beautiful part of Punjab, bought an estate there, and married a local woman. The widowed lady was now writing to Ronald, whom she had known during her husband's lifetime. She wrote making him an offer the nature of which was unclear and Ronald therefore asked the Kazini to correspond with her on his behalf and sort things out. The fact was that on her husband's death the Lady of Kulu had inherited the estate and she wanted that on her own death it should go to Ronald. It had come to her from an Englishman, so she declared, and it was right that it should go back to an Englishman. Whether this involved Ronald marrying her I never knew. I knew only that he had moved to the Kulu Valley and was living on the estate with the lady. According to the Kazini, to whom Ronald wrote more about the business than he did to me, they were not happy together and quarrelled violently. Though the lady was seventy-five (this may have been one of the Kazini's little exaggerations) she wanted to be told she was still beautiful, and Ronald found it difficult to do this. She died, however, and Ronald came into possession of the estate. Unfortunately, the lady's nephew and niece, who had expected to inherit the estate themselves, accused him of having murdered their aunt. He was arrested, kept in prison, in shackles, and it was many months before he could be released, there being no evidence against him. As he may well have reflected, his stay in the Kulu Valley had gone far more amiss than had the Kazini's stay in Kalimpong.

Chapter Four

THE OLD BHUTAN PALACE

THERE ARE PEOPLE with whom we become friends at the first meeting, and others with whom we become friends only after knowing
them for a long time. Similarly, there are gurus with whom we immediately form a strong spiritual connection, others with whom we
develop such a connection only gradually. In my own case, Chattrul
Rimpoche was an example of the first kind of guru, Dhardo
Rimpoche of the second.

Dhardo Rimpoche was a monk of the Gelug school, also known as
the Yellow Hats on account of the yellow pandit hats they wore for
certain ceremonial purposes, as distinct from the red hats worn by
members of the three other schools of Tibetan Buddhism. As it happened, Dhardo Rimpoche set eyes on me before I set eyes on him. I
was then in Bodh Gaya, where the Buddha had attained Enlightenment, staying at the Maha Bodhi Society's rest house. Rimpoche was
staying at the nearby Tibetan gompa, of which he had recently been
appointed abbot by the Tibetan government. Looking out of the
window of his room one day, he espied me on the flat roof of the rest
house. So astonished was he to see an Englishman in yellow monastic robes that he called to his attendant.

'Look!' he exclaimed, 'the Dharma has gone as far as the West!'

This was in 1949, and it was not until 1952 that we actually met.
There had recently been a dispute in Bodh Gaya between Dhardo
Rimpoche and the young Sinhalese monk who ran the Maha Bodhi
Society's rest house, and the authorities of the Society, knowing that
the Rimpoche was now back in Kalimpong, had asked me to see him
about the matter. This I was glad to do, as I did not want the dispute

to develop into a permanent breach between the Tibetan Buddhists and the Maha Bodhi Society. The next morning, therefore, I set out for Tirpai, where the Gelug lama was staying, taking with me as my interpreter a highly intelligent young Tibetan whom I had known for a year or more. This was Lobsang Phuntsok Lhalungpa, a former monk official, who was a close associate of Dhardo Rimpoche and anxious that I should meet him. The Rimpoche occupied the first floor of Sherpa Building, the ground floor being occupied by Joe Cann, who on the strength of his having given the Rimpoche a few English lessons had developed a rather proprietary attitude towards him and had assured me, on more than one occasion, that he was far too important and busy a lama to have time for me. Dhardo Rimpoche did, however, have time for me. In fact, he was very pleased to see me, especially as he recognized in me the yellow-robed figure he had seen on the roof of the Maha Bodhi Society's rest house in Bodh Gaya.

After we had exchanged the usual amenities, I told the Rimpoche the reason for my visit. He at once became very serious, and proceeded to give me a full account of the dispute between himself and the young Sinhalese monk, who I knew to be hot-headed and given to using intemperate language. As the Rimpoche spoke, I received such an impression of sheer goodwill, candour, and integrity that when I wrote to the General Secretary of the Maha Bodhi Society the following morning I had no hesitation in assuring him that Dhardo Rimpoche was in no way at fault and that the blame for the dispute rested solely with the Sinhalese monk.

Thus began a friendship that lasted for the rest of my time in India, and which did not cease with my departure for England. It was a friendship in the course of which Dhardo Rimpoche and I worked closely together for the good of Buddhism, especially in Kalimpong. It was a friendship which culminated, moreover, in my receiving from him the Bodhisattva ordination in 1962 and the White Tara 'long-life' initiation the following year, so that from being my friend he became also my teacher.

In 1954 Dhardo Rimpoche moved to the Old Bhutan Palace, and it was there that we had our second meeting. He was then thirty-six, which meant that he was my senior by seven years. Of medium height, and rather slightly built, he wore an informal 'indoor' version of monastic dress consisting of a fawn underskirt and a sleeveless shirt of orange silk. His black hair was cropped instead of his being shaven-headed like a Theravadin monk, and a few long hairs on his upper lip gave promise of a whispy moustache. The Rimpoche spoke very little English, but he had command of a fluent if ungrammatical Hindi, and it was in that language that we conversed. During the years in which we were in personal contact there developed between us a sort of patois in which our common Hindi was freely mixed with English words and phrases as well as Tibetan, and even Sanskrit, religious and philosophical terms. Thus we were able to discuss almost any subject, from politics to the doctrine of voidness, and from sadhana practice to the production of books and pamphlets. Such discussion was facilitated by the fact that there was in our communication an intuitive element, almost telepathic in its nature, that supplemented, or even bypassed, the words we spoke.

At our first meeting Dhardo Rimpoche had been serious, as befitted the matter I had come to discuss with him. On the present occasion, too, he was serious, but in a more animated way and with regard to a subject of a very different kind. This subject was the school he was planning to start. Lobsang Lhalungpa, Pheunkhangsey, and others were helping him, and the school would be housed there in the Old Bhutan Palace, on the upper floor of which he was now living. The huge, rather ramshackle wooden building had, it seemed, been placed at his disposal by Rani Chunni Dorji, the wife (later widow) of Raja S. T. Dorji, the effective Prime Minister of Bhutan and Kalimpong's leading Buddhist citizen. The school would teach Tibetan and Buddhism in the morning, Dhardo Rimpoche explained, and modern subjects in the afternoon. There were many refugee children in Kalimpong, and he was anxious that they should grow up with a knowledge of their own religion and culture. At the same time, he realized that they had to be equipped to meet the demands of life in the modern world. From the way in which he spoke I could see that he had the interests of the children very much at heart, besides being deeply concerned for the preservation of the language, literature, and religion of his native land.

It was in the course of this meeting, I think, that Dhardo Rimpoche invited me to cooperate with him in establishing the Indo-Tibetan Buddhist Cultural Institute School, as it came rather grandly to be called, and to give a series of fortnightly lectures under its auspices. Both invitations I was happy to accept. I do not remember how many lectures I gave, but I gave them at the Old Bhutan Palace itself, in a large room on the upper floor where the Thirteenth Dalai Lama had once stayed. Thereafter I was a regular visitor to the school whenever I was not out on tour and when Dhardo Rimpoche himself was not in Bodh Gaya. This meant quite a long walk for me, as the Old Bhutan Palace was situated some distance beyond the bazaar, below the road that led, eventually, to Lhasa. From this road a broad track paved with cobbles as big as small boulders led down to an open space that had once been the Palace courtyard and was now the school playground. On my arrival I would be given tea, and the Rimpoche and I would talk. He might then show me what was happening in the different classrooms, or ask me to translate a letter. From time to time he came to see me at my own place, usually bringing with him something for me to type, in which case he also brought his own stationery and carbon paper. On such occasions he wore the usual maroon monastic dress, and his faithful monk attendant Gelong Lobsang, who accompanied him wherever he went, followed a few steps behind. Lobsang was younger than his master, but looked older. He had stiff black hair which, since he did not keep it very short, stuck out from his head on all sides. His habitual expression was one of extreme dourness, but sometimes, as when a remark was addressed to him, his face would light up with a delightful smile.

In 1956 Buddhism was 2,500 years old, reckoning from the date of the Buddha's *parinirvana* or 'final passing away', and the occasion was celebrated all over the Buddhist world. Though India was not a Buddhist country, the Buddha Jayanti, as it was called, was widely celebrated here too. Indeed, it received official patronage and support on cultural grounds, much to the disgust of some orthodox Caste Hindus. As part of the celebrations, some fifty representatives of the Buddhists of Ladakh, Sikkim, Assam, the North-East Frontier Agency, and so on were invited to tour the holy placed as guests of the Government of India and to spend four days in Delhi in that capacity. Both Dhardo Rimpoche and I were among the invitees, presumably as representing the Buddhists of Kalimpong. The Eminent Buddhists from the Border Areas, as we were officially styled, were given a special train, where we ate and slept, and from which we were taken every day by coach to either a holy place or an important government project. In this way we visited Bodh Gaya, Rajgir, Nalanda, Sarnath, Kusinara, Lumbini, and Sanchi, all of which I had seen before, as well as several huge dams that were under construction. We also visited Agra, where I saw the Taj Mahal for the first time. In Delhi we met the President, Dr Rajendra Prasad; met the Vice-President, Dr Radhakrishnan; had lunch at the Prime Minister's house, where Pandit Nehru took me into the garden and showed me his giant pandas, and were among the tens of thousands who gathered at the airport to welcome the youthful Dalai Lama (with whom I later had a private interview) and the no less youthful Panchen Lama.

During the week that we were on tour, and the four days we were in Delhi, Dhardo Rimpoche and I occupied the same compartment in the train, which we shared with my Sikkimese friend Sonam Topgay and with S. Yhonzone, a young Tamang Buddhist from Kurseong, a small hill station near Darjeeling, with whom I was already acquainted. Living as we did in such close proximity, sharing meals and going on excursions together, the four of us naturally got to know one another better than we might otherwise have done. I certainly got to know Dhardo Rimpoche better. I saw that he was adaptable, that he did not stand on his dignity as an incarnate lama (it was the first time he had travelled without Gelong Lobsang), and that he had a lively sense of humour. Above all, I saw how uniformly kind he was, how unfailingly mindful. His mindfulness consisted not merely in an absence of anything resembling forgetfulness or inattention, but also in a degree of foresight and preparedness that was almost supernatural.

There occurred an incident which strikingly exemplified this particular quality of his. It was the custom of the officials who were looking after the party and organizing its transport to tell us which places we would be visiting that day. One morning they told us we would be visiting a certain dam in the morning, and in the afternoon, after returning to the train for lunch, a certain holy place. Unfortunately there was somehow a mix-up. An hour after leaving the train we found ourselves not at the dam, as we had expected, but at the holy place. This in itself did not really matter, but thinking we would not be needing them until the afternoon none of us had brought any candles or incense sticks. None of us, that is, except Dhardo Rimpoche. As we were lamenting the fact that we would be unable to offer worship in the proper manner, he produced packets of candles and bundles of incense sticks from beneath his voluminous robes and smilingly distributed them among us. As I was to say in later years, Dhardo Rimpoche was never caught napping.

Back in Kalimpong, both the Rimpoche and I had work to do. In his case, besides having the school to run, which was quite a responsibility, he had to decide what was to be done about Ani-la. It was two years since the turbulent Frenchwoman had cut off contact with him. During that period she had behaved more and more outrageously, so that she was now notorious throughout the district and was bringing the whole Buddhist community into disrepute. Since she refused to come and see him, he felt he had no alternative but to deprive her of the *getsulma* or 'female novice' ordination he had conferred on her four years earlier, and in July 1958 he drew up a document to this effect. With his help, I produced an English version of this document, a copy of which, signed and sealed by him, was to be given to his erstwhile disciple. In it Dhardo Rimpoche declared that she had been proved guilty of grave offences against the monastic law, that by virtue of the authority vested in him by the Dalai Lama he was depriving her of her ordination, and that she was no longer entitled to the support of the lay community. Ten offences were enumerated. She had refused to submit herself to the lawful monastic authorities; had openly blasphemed the Holy Dharma; had grossly slandered sundry incarnate lamas and members of the Sangha; had gravely slandered prominent lay persons of the locality; had declared in writing that she was not a Buddhist and that she was wearing the monastic robe for the sake of worldly acquisition; had publicly declared her intention of writing a book against Buddhism; had misappropriated religious books; had been guilty of an act of violence; had conducted herself publicly in an unseemly manner; and had by her behaviour been a source of scandal and brought the whole Buddhist community into contempt and disrespect.

Unfortunately, all this was not only true but also a matter of public knowledge, and even of public record, as in the case of the scathing article on Himalayan Buddhism that Ani-la had published in the town's little English weekly paper. Some of her offences had been committed in front of me, as well as in front of others, and some she herself told me about. Among the latter was the act of violence of which she had been guilty. The act had been committed in Darjeeling. The taxi she had ordered having arrived late, she struck the driver a blow in the face with her fist, knocking out two front teeth. She apologized to him afterwards, and gave him a tin of fifty cigarettes by way of compensation. The incident was an ugly one, and the police had become involved. A European had assaulted an Indian. What was more, the perpetrator of the assault was a Buddhist nun. In telling me about the incident, Ani-la pleaded extenuating circumstances, saying that she had arranged to meet a visiting French scholar at his hotel, and the taxi was to have taken her there. By making her late for her appointment the driver had lowered her in the eyes of her compatriot, who would think her an uncivilized person, and this thought so infuriated her that when the driver at last appeared she had lashed out at him. As she was a strong, sturdy woman, a blow from her fist was no light matter, and I was not surprised that it should have knocked out two of the unfortunate man's teeth. The Kazini Sahiba, to whom the French Nun was able to pour out her troubles in her own language, was of the opinion that she had the physique of a peasant and that Nature had meant her to do hard farm work and have lots of babies. She was also convinced that Ani-la's talk of suicide could not be taken seriously, especially in view of what the latter had once told her. It had been one of those times when, feeling deeply depressed and thinking that life was not worth living, she had walked into the forests of western Sikkim with the intention of committing suicide there.

'But you know what these cheap Bata shoes are like,' she told the Kazini, 'I hadn't gone very far when they started leaking. So I turned back.'

The Kazini found the idea of someone being prevented from committing suicide by leaking shoes quite ludicrous, and she could not help smiling as she told me the story. For my part, I found the incident not only ludicrous but pathetic, and despite her bad behaviour I felt sorry for the French Nun. Her life in Kalimpong had begun so well! From being a student of Hindu temple architecture and Sanskrit she had become first a Theravadin anagarika or 'homeless one' and then a getsulma or novice nun. It was evident from the beginning, however, that she was by nature extremely demanding, so that if what she considered to be her legitimate intellectual and spiritual needs were not met, or not met in the way she wanted, her face would assume an aggrieved, sullen, resentful expression, and sooner or later there would be an explosion. I witnessed several such explosions, and heard about others (sometimes from the aggrieved party herself, if she was in a repentant mood), for even those who were most anxious to help Ani-la did not find it easy to do so and consequently incurred her wrath. I used to say of her that she would ask a guru to teach her as she prostrated herself before him, then tell him just how he ought to do this as she rose to her feet, which was in fact not far from the truth. Naturally she was disappointed, and this led to her becoming increasingly frustrated, disillusioned, and bitter, and more and more inclined to blame everyone for her unhappiness except herself. Her behaviour also changed, especially after she left Kachu Rimpoche, eventually becoming so much at variance with the kind of behaviour expected of a Buddhist nun that Dhardo Rimpoche was obliged to take action against her.

Dhardo Rimpoche might deprive Ani-la of her ordination, and even draw up a document to that effect, but he could not compel her to stop wearing the monastic robe, as he would have been able to do in Tibet. Indeed, he found it difficult to get a copy of the English version of the document delivered to her. He therefore decided to hand it to her himself. On learning that she was visiting friends at the Himalayan Hotel, he took up position beside the front gate and waited for her to emerge, thinking that when she did so he would speak to her and get her to accept the document. When she did at length emerge, however, she rudely thrust him aside as he attempted to greet her and proceeded on her way without a word. I was deeply pained when I heard how Ani-la had behaved towards Dhardo Rimpoche, who had treated her so kindly and endured her vagaries with such patience. The picture of him standing beside the front gate of the hotel, waiting for her in the darkness, haunted my imagination for a long time. The Rimpoche himself did not complain, but he must have wondered how an educated European woman could act so rudely. In Tibet, one was expected to treat everybody, even an enemy, with the courtesy that was due from one human being to another. Good manners were part of Buddhist ethics.

Grave as were the offences Ani-la had committed, and for which she had been deprived of her ordination, one of the worst things she did found no place in Dhardo Rimpoche's document and was not, I think, known to him. It was in connection with George Roerich, the Russian Tibetologist, who lived in some style in a mock-Tudor villa in the best part of Kalimpong. Ani-la had once asked him to teach her Tibetan. He had refused, and since then she had borne him a grudge. One day she came to see me, breathless and trembling with excitement. She had discovered Roerich's secret, she announced triumphantly, her eyes gleaming. She had found out where his money came from. The story, as she then proceeded to tell it to me, was that she had been eating in a restaurant in the bazaar when she heard two men talking on the other side of the partition separating her banquette from theirs. They were talking in Tibetan. More than two years had passed since Roerich's refusal to teach her, and during that period she had acquired enough colloquial Tibetan to be able to follow their conversation. They had come from Mongolia, she gathered; they had some gold with them, and the gold was meant for Roerich. Having told me all this, she declared her intention of going to Chandralok, the tall, isolated building that housed the area headquarters of the Central Intelligence Bureau, and telling them what she had learned. I strongly advised her not to get mixed up in the business, but she refused to listen. Roerich had refused to teach her Tibetan, she reminded me, and now she was going to have her revenge. And off she went to Chandralok as fast as her legs could carry her. A week later I heard that Roerich had suddenly left Kalimpong. When next heard of, he was in Moscow.

I do not remember how long it was after Roerich's departure that Ani-la, too, disappeared from the scene. For the few weeks that she remained in the area after being deprived of her ordination she continued to wear the monastic robe, but when next heard of she was in Calcutta, where she was seen with bobbed hair, in a short skirt, and puffing a cigarette.

Chapter Five

THE SECRET ORDER OF THE POTALA

WHEN I MOVED into the stone cottage that was to become the Triyana Vardhana Vihara, some of my friends wondered what I would do with the four acres of terraced hillside land that went with it. I had no experience of gardening, let alone of farming. But I told them not to worry. If an uneducated Nepalese or Lepcha peasant could grow crops, I was sure I could do so. Give me a year, I said, and I would know as much as any of them.

The property's most valuable asset, apart from the cottage, were its orange trees, of which there were about a hundred. The trees had been neglected by the previous owners and stood in need of some attention. I therefore had the soil round each one of them loosened, care being taken not to damage the roots, and manure dug in. The oranges were of the small, sweet, easily peeled variety that in my childhood appeared in the shops at Christmas time and were known as tangerines. They were grown throughout the Kalimpong subdivision, as well as in Sikkim, and were an important cash crop. As soon as the trees had fruited the middlemen would come round, going from orchard to orchard and buying up the entire crop in advance, except for the two or three trees one reserved for one's own consumption. The secret was not to accept the first offer that was made but to wait until the orange season was in full swing and the wholesale price had peaked. Some orange growers could not afford to wait, and the middleman, taking advantage of their need for ready money, would drive a hard bargain. During my time at the Vihara the price I got for my oranges rose steadily, so that the price I got for them in 1964 was ten times what in had been in 1957. I also started growing buckwheat between the orange trees. Its crimson stalks and pink-and-white flowers created a sea of colour out of which the trees seemed to rise.

So far as I remember, the buckwheat was not sold. The crop was never a big one, and in any case the other community members and I all enjoyed our Lepcha cook's fried buckwheat cakes. We did have another cash crop besides the oranges, however. This was maize or Indian corn, locally known as *makkai*. It was cultivated for us by a sharecropper inherited from the previous owners of the property, and thanks to his labour the handsome plant with the long green leaves and purple-tasselled pods covered more than two-thirds of the land. The sharecropper was a bent, shambling old Nepalese brahmin with yellow, decaying teeth and a long, thick *tiki* or ritual crown lock that hung half way down his back. He liked to come and chat with me from time to time, squatting on the veranda in his dirty clothes, and smelling of sweat, manure, and cheap country tobacco. At first I used to offer him tea, but he always refused, as our cook was a non-brahmin and the caste-conscious old man would not accept even water from his hand. As he was by birth a member of the priestly cast, he was invariably addressed by Hindus and Buddhists alike as Bhaje, which meant something like 'your worship'. This did not mean he was always treated with deference. 'Come here, Bhaje, you old rascal,' someone might shout to him.

When the year's makkai crop had been divided equally between us, I would sell the greater part of the Vihara's share of the pods, the rest being stored in a sort of miniature haystack mounted on stilts. This kept them out of the reach of rats. The haystacks were of two kinds, the round and the oblong, the Nepalese and the Lepcha, though which kind was associated with which community I no longer remember. When one wanted a few pods, all one had to do was reach up and pull them out of the stack. Coarsely ground, the parti-coloured grain could be made into a sort of porridge, so that we had no need to buy packaged breakfast cereals. There was also plenty of corn on the cob to eat, especially early in the season when the grain was small, soft, and sweet.

Growing vegetables was a matter of trial and error, as I quickly discovered. The soil, which was full of mica, did not suit either potatoes or cauliflowers. Such potatoes as we managed to produce were hardly bigger than marbles, while our cauliflowers were not only stunted but preyed upon by caterpillars to such an extent that their leaves were reduced to skeletons. The pumpkin, on the other hand, required little or no attention and was extremely prolific. One was always coming across fruit hidden beneath the big leaves, and the plant's tender leading shoots made an excellent green vegetable. The *kadela*, or bitter gourd, was no less prolific. It bore tiny yellow flowers, and the green, crinkled gourds, rarely more than six inches in length, dangled at the end of a long string by which it was connected with the parent vine. As it ripened, it became a beautiful golden yellow colour, eventually bursting open to reveal brilliant scarlet seeds. Both the flowers and the dangling gourds themselves emitted a strange aroma that I found not unpleasing.

The banana trees and the bamboos, like the pumpkin, required little or no attention. There were thirty or more bamboos, all thick as a man's arm and rising to a height of thirty or forty feet. They grew close together, so that when the wind blew, and the slender tops nodded, they knocked against one another, producing sounds that were almost musical. Since the bamboo is a species of grass, they died and grew afresh every year. In the rainy season they grew with great rapidity, as did the banana trees and the makkai, sometimes achieving as much as eight or nine inches of growth in a single night. There was a constant demand for bamboos in the locality. They were used in building construction, sections of them could be made into vessels for drinking home-brewed beer, and split lengthwise they were the means by which water could be channelled from a higher to a lower terrace, in a process sometimes even crossing the road high overhead. Hence there were few weeks that I did not sell a bamboo to a neighbour, who would chop it down himself with his kukri and march away with it balanced on his shoulder.

The Bamboo Grove, as I liked to call it, was situated a little beyond the orange trees, on a lower terrace. I used to go down from time to time and stand among the bamboos admiring their smooth greenness, inhaling the smell of the fallen leaves underfoot and, if there was a breeze, listening to the sounds they made as they knocked against one another. Once, on my way down to the terrace, I caught sight of a strange bird in the grove. About the size of a pheasant, it was a deep emerald green from its head to the tip of its long tail. By the time I reached the grove it had disappeared and I never saw it again. None of the people to whom I described it could tell me what it was, and some of my friends thought I must have imagined it. Real or a product of my imagination, to me the mysterious bird was the spirit of the Bamboo Grove, even of the little hillside property itself.

'If you have a loaf of bread,' the prophet of Islam is reported as saying, 'sell half and buy a rose.' The Vihara had plenty of oranges and plenty of makkai, but I also needed flowers for the shrine-room, where I meditated each morning and evening and where members and friends of the Vihara celebrated the full moon days. But at the time I moved in, the only flowers to be seen were the small pink-and-yellow ones on the lantana bushes bordering the property. I therefore created a little garden on the terrace immediately below the cottage, and soon we had plenty of French marigolds and zinnias, besides a few gerberas, which Tibetan friends told me had been the favourite flowers of the Thirteenth Dalai Lama. I had half a dozen big flowerpots made, grew geraniums in them from cuttings, and placed them at intervals along the veranda. On the steep bank behind the cottage I created a kind of 'orchidarium'. Exotic and expensive as orchids might have been in Europe, in the part of the world in which I now lived they grew in abundance, and were little regarded by the local people. If one wanted a few plants, all one had to do was to send a man into the forest with a *tokri*, the big, cone-shaped wicker basket in which the Nepalese, men and women alike, carried loads on their backs. He would climb up into the trees and gather the plants until he had a full *tokri*.

This was dangerous work, for the orchids grew high on the trees, preferring branches that were rotten and therefore unsafe. Hence there were two ways of paying the man. One could either give him two rupees, and pay his family a hundred rupees if he fell from the tree and was killed, or one could give him five rupees and be free from any such liability. I opted for the first alternative, sent a man into the forest one morning, and by the evening had several dozen plants. These I attached to bits of rotten wood, then thrust the wood into holes that had been dug in the bank behind the cottage. Before many months had passed, long sprays of orchids appeared from among the green leaves, some snowy white, some golden yellow. They were the most common varieties, knowledgeable friends told me. Joe Cann in particular was very dismissive of my orchids. *He* had some extremely rare specimens, he assured me, for which he had paid a lot of money. But I did not care. I loved orchids, as I loved all other flowers, for their beauty, not for their rarity or their monetary value.

The orange trees and the makkai, the vegetables and the flowers, all required a certain amount of attention from me, even if this meant only that I directed the labour of others. The work of the farmer and the gardener was never done, it appeared, even when the area under cultivation was no more than four acres. Yet there was at least one project which I began soon after moving into the property and succeeded in finishing shortly afterwards. This was the construction of a five-roomed guest cottage. I had always had visitors from distant places, and I had usually been able to put them up for a night or two at the rented premises I happened to be occupying at the time. The stone cottage that was the Vihara proper was quite small, and though a visiting monk might be accommodated in the shrine-room and other guests in a loft above what had once been a cowshed, something better was badly needed. I therefore decided to build. There was no question of my building in stone, which would have been difficult and expensive; but there was no reason why I should not build with wood and bamboo, as the villagers did. For this I had the means and, I hoped, the capacity.

First I drew a ground plan of the building, and decided on its dimensions. I then hired a carpenter, discussed with him what materials would be needed, and sent him to the bazaar to buy wood and to hire four coolies. A site adjacent to the Vihara having been levelled, the foundations of the cottage were laid and the work of construction could begin. I have no recollection of the different stages of the work, but it progressed steadily, and by the end of the second week the wooden frame of the cottage stood complete. At the time I was busy, as I usually was, writing articles and book reviews, but every half hour or so I would leave my desk and go outside to see what my workmen were doing. The Nepalese carpenter, Lal Bahadur, who acted as foreman, was a good worker, but the coolies slacked or disappeared if an eye was not kept on them. The frame of the cottage being in place, the spaces between the vertical and lateral beams of the outer and inner walls had to be filled in with what in

England would have been called wattle-and-daub, the 'wattle' being split bamboo and the 'daub' clay mixed with chopped jute sacking. This work was done by the coolies, while Lal Bahadur got on with making doors, window frames, and beds. Finding the reeds with which the cottage was to be thatched proved difficult. Reeds were in short supply, it seemed, and in the end they had to be brought up from somewhere near Teesta Bridge by bullock cart. They came in bundles which, laid side by side in layers, made a roof a foot thick. It would last for three years, I was told. In fact it lasted for the rest of my time in Kalimpong. All that now remained for Lal Bahadur to do was to hang the doors and glaze the windows. This having been done, the walls of the cottage were whitewashed, and the doors and windows painted bright yellow.

It was the local custom that on the completion of a house the builder should give the workmen a feast on the site. I had no objection to going along with this custom. Thanks to my five workmen, the Vihara now had a five-roomed guest cottage capable of accommodating eight persons. The work had proceeded smoothly; the cottage had been built in a month, and it had cost me just over a thousand rupees, which was a little more than a twentieth of what I had given for the stone cottage and its four acres of hillside land. But though I had no objection to giving the workmen their feast, I declined to provide the customary meat and liquor. Lal Bahadur and the four coolies had a merry time nonetheless, chatting and laughing, and eating as much food as they could. On their departure I gave them some extra money, which they no doubt spent on liquor in the bazaar.

The Vihara's modest guest cottage was occupied, over the years, by a number of people. One of the earliest of them, and the most unusual, was a visitor who arrived unexpectedly in the summer of 1958. I was in my sitting-room one morning, reading, when I was told there was a sahib to see me. He was tall and heavily bearded, and carried a pipe. Over a cup of tea he said he had come from Bodh Gaya, from Dhardo Rimpoche, who had told him that the English monk in Kalimpong would be able to teach him what he wanted to know. The Rimpoche had been wearing a skirt, he added, laughing uproariously, as if the idea of a man wearing a skirt was the funniest thing in the world. What, then did he want to know, I enquired, when the guffaws had subsided. He wanted to know how to read people's thoughts, he replied unhesitatingly, and how to see what was happening at a distance. But before I could ask him why he wanted to acquire those powers he produced a newspaper cutting from his wallet and silently handed it to me. From it I learned that my bearded, pipe-smoking visitor was in fact a woman. Born in 1915, he had been orphaned at an early age, had been brought up by two maiden aunts, had gone to Oxford, and between 1945 and 1948 had undergone a series of operations that had given him the outward appearance of a man, thus enabling him to pass as such. He had then qualified as a doctor, and until recently had worked as a ship's doctor on a British liner, resigning only when the discovery of his change of sex by a reporter had led to its extensive coverage in the press. The press was still on his trail, he explained, though he believed he had shaken them off in Calcutta. Could he stay at the Vihara until things had blown over? I assured him he could stay as long as he wished. Within half an hour of his arrival, therefore, my unusual visitor had been installed in the guest house and was arranging his scanty belongings. To make it difficult for the press to track him down he shaved off his beard and I gave him a Buddhist name, so that Michael (née Laura) Dillon became Jivaka, which had been the name of Buddha's personal physician.

Later he told me he had been greatly impressed by the fact that I had read the newspaper cutting without turning a hair, as he put it, as well as by the readiness with which I had agreed to his staying at the Vihara. If I did not turn a hair on learning of Jivaka's sex-change, it was partly because I was familiar with the phenomenon from my reading of the Buddhist scriptures, where it was represented as occurring spontaneously. In Jivaka's case the change had not occurred spontaneously but as the result of a series of surgical operations. He liked to talk about these operations, of which there had been thirty-six, spread over a period of three years. They had begun with the removal of his unwanted breasts, two semicircular scars being still visible when he went bare-chested in hot weather. The plastic surgeon who had carried out the operations was a pioneer in the field, I gathered, and it was evident that Jivaka regarded him with admiration and gratitude. He was especially grateful for his artificial penis, of which he was immensely proud. One day he offered to show it to me, assuring me that it was 'a beautiful piece of work'; but I declined the offer. Despite all the operations he had undergone, however, Jivaka's change of sex was far from being either complete or final. He was still having to take hormone tablets to promote the growth of facial hair and suppress menstruation. The change from female to male would in fact never be complete. Jivaka was essentially a woman whom modern surgical techniques and modern drugs had enabled to act the part of a man on the stage of life. The beard, the pipe, and so on, were all so many stage props. There were times when he overacted the part, as when he laughed uproariously at the idea of a man wearing a skirt. At other times he could behave like an overgrown schoolboy, as when he astonished other members of the community, who thought he had gone mad, by suddenly gyrating up and down on the veranda, waving a letter and shouting at the top of his voice, 'Oxford's won the Boat Race! Oxford's won the Boat Race!' For although he had gone to Oxford before having his mastectomy, and had belonged to one of the women's colleges, he thought of himself as being very much an 'Oxford man'.

The fact that he was the first female-to-male transsexual to have modern surgery and hormone treatment was not the most interesting thing about Jivaka, at least so far as I was concerned. He was also a disciple of the notorious Lobsang Rampa, author of the best-selling *The Third Eye*, who was not a Tibetan lama at all but a plumber from Plympton with a vivid imagination and a racy style. A few weeks after his arrival at the Vihara, Jivaka confided to me, with a solemn air, that Lobsang Rampa had initiated him into the Secret Order of the Potala and invested him with its robe and girdle. There were only thirteen members of the Order, including the Dalai Lama, and every Tibetan who saw him wearing the robe – however highly placed – would immediately prostrate himself before him. He had worn the robe when he went to see Dhardo Rimpoche, he added, but strange to say, the Rimpoche had not prostrated himself. Perhaps he was a low-ranking lama who had not heard of the Secret Order of the Potala.

Naturally I wanted to know if Jivaka had brought the robe with him. He indeed had, he assured me, and at my request not only showed it to me but demonstrated how it was to be worn, wrapping it round himself in the most extraordinary fashion and tying it with what appeared to be a length of dressing-gown cord.

'But Jivaka, it's an ordinary Burmese monk's robe!' I exclaimed, with genuine astonishment.

'No, it's not,' he retorted angrily. 'It's the robe of the Secret Order of the Potala.'

Fortunately I had just such a monk's robe in my cupboard, presented to me by Burmese pilgrims whom I had met in one of the holy places. It was of the same yellowish-brown colour as the one Jivaka was wearing, consisted of the same number of patches, and bore in one corner the same manufacturer's label in Burmese script.

Jivaka was dumbfounded by the discovery. Even so, I had a hard time convincing him that Lobsang Rampa was not, as he claimed, a lama who had spent many years in Lhasa and been initiated into the deepest mysteries of Tibetan Buddhism, and that the Secret Order of the Potala existed only in his fertile imagination. Eventually, however, I did convince him, whereupon he wrote to Rampa, who was then living in Ireland in a house bought for him by Jivaka, a letter of indignant remonstrance. To this the supposed lama only replied that evidently some evil person had been undermining his faith.

Jivaka's faith in his erstwhile master was indeed undermined, but not his faith in his own high spiritual destiny – a faith that had enabled him to regard membership of the Secret Order of the Potala as being no more than his due.

'I *know* that I am a teacher, a teacher with a capital T,' he told me not long after his disillusionment with Rampa.

'In that case you ought to have something to teach,' I responded, not without irony.

Jivaka failed to notice the irony. 'I never thought of that,' he said, quite seriously.

What a teacher ought to have, he seems to have thought, were psychic powers – especially a teacher with a capital T. This was why he wanted to be able to read people's thoughts and how to see what was happening at a distance. For on my asking him, earlier, why he wanted to know these things he had replied that it was because they would be helpful to him in his work. What that work was he refused to tell me, only observing, rather portentously, that when the time came for it to be known I would know it. That time had now come, it seemed. By his work he had meant his work as a Teacher, for that was what he 'knew' himself to be. Later he went so far as to speak in a mysterious, oracular manner that suggested he believed he was a reincarnation of Jesus Christ. In the meantime, however, his energies were being applied to the study of Buddhism. A Teacher ought to have something to teach!

As I had discovered soon after his arrival, Jivaka was acquainted with the ideas of Gurdjieff and Ouspensky, but he knew nothing about Buddhism, least of all about Tibetan Buddhism, despite – or perhaps because of – his association with Lobsang Rampa. I had a small Buddhist library, and from this I selected books for him to read, mark, learn and, I hoped, inwardly digest. He certainly read them (he was a very fast reader), and he may have marked and learned to an extent, but nothing was inwardly digested. It was as though what he read went straight into his head without passing through his heart. He had no understanding of the need for reflection and assimilation, especially in the case of the Buddhist scriptures, and he grumbled that I doled out books to him instead of allowing him the run of my library. He also grumbled about the hard wooden bed, about the monotonous vegetarian diet, and about the difficulty of sitting cross-legged for the morning and evening puja and meditation. Nonetheless he was cheerful, perhaps even happy, for he had escaped the press and was living quietly in a Buddhist monastery which he seemed increasingly disposed to regard as home. At any rate, despite my being ten years younger than himself, he insisted on calling me 'Daddy', which I heartily disliked. Beneath the outsized pseudo-masculinity, the wilfulness, and the spiritual ambition, I detected, I thought, a rather infantile craving for affection.

Jivaka not only read fast; he also wrote fast. Letters poured from his pen, all addressed to the few friends in England who knew of his sex-change and who could be trusted not to reveal his whereabouts to the press. Articles also poured from his pen, as did an autobiography to which he gave the title *Out of the Ordinary*. It was written at my suggestion, and later he returned the compliment by suggesting that I, too, should write my autobiography. His life had indeed been an extraordinary one, and reading about it was an interesting experience. I could not but be impressed by the courage and tenacity he had shown, however misguidedly, in choosing to undergo a series of difficult, painful, and potentially dangerous operations, and I asked him why he had been so desperately anxious to change his sex. There were two reasons, he replied. One reason was that he had always felt that he was a male soul trapped in a female body, and he wanted to bring his body into line with his soul. The other was that he was sexually attracted to women and thought that if he had a male instead of a female body 'it would be all right', the implication being that lesbianism was immoral and therefore out of the question. He did not say if it ever had been 'all right', and in the autobiography there was no mention of any sexual relationship.

'He's a strange man, your Jivaka,' one day remarked the Kazini, to whom I had introduced the Vihara's new guest and to whom he was indebted for the occasional non-vegetarian meal. 'There's something wrong with him but I can't put my finger on it. It's as though his sex had gone rotten within him.'

She was a very perceptive woman, and for a moment I thought she must have guessed Jivaka's secret. But she had not, which was fortunate, for she would have found it difficult to keep such a titillating piece of information to herself.

The future transsexual's childhood had been an unhappy one, the autobiography made clear. The two elderly maiden aunts who had brought him up were women of narrow, conventional views who had sought to mould the tomboyish girl, as Jivaka then was, into an upper-class young lady who would make a good marriage. Both aunts were extremely miserly. Though they had sizeable private incomes, they had somehow managed to convince themselves that they were very poor and barely able to afford necessaries. Reading about their curious, penny-pinching ways, I could not help wondering if Jivaka had inherited something of his aunts' attitude to money. It had been agreed at the beginning of his stay that the Vihara should charge him five rupees a day for his board and lodging (the Himalayan Hotel charged twenty), but he seemed to think that the one hundred and fifty rupees to which this amounted each month was a huge sum, and that he was being incredibly generous in paying so much.

Jivaka had not been with us for many months when I left for a preaching tour of central and western India. On my return I found that during my absence there had been serious trouble between

Jivaka and Dupchen Lama, one of the younger members of the community. Dupchen was from the Duars, a densely forested area that marched with the southern border of Bhutan and formed part of Assam. I had gone there at the invitation of the local Tamang Buddhists, some of whom were concerned that they knew so little about their ancestral faith. Besides giving Dharma talks and holding discussions, I suggested they should give me a young man to teach and train at my monastery in Kalimpong. To this they readily agreed, and I chose a bright-faced young man of about twenty who had listened to my Dharma talks with particular interest and had already expressed a wish to study with me. He would join me in Kalimpong in three weeks time, his family promised.

Three weeks later there arrived at the Vihara a small, scared boy of ten or eleven. It was Dupchen. He brought with him a letter from his uncle, who informed me that the young man I had chosen was not able to come, after all, and that he was sending Dupchen in his place. Though I was disappointed and suspected I was being taken advantage of, I did not have the heart to send the boy back to the Duars, especially after learning that he was an orphan and that his uncle, with whom he had been living, did not want to have any further responsibility for him. I therefore assigned him a room in the guest cottage, and had him admitted to the local government boys' school.

He was not very bright, and did not do well at school. More than once I had to discuss his lack of progress with the headmaster, whom I happened to know. But Dupchen seemed happy enough. He had friends both at school and at the Vihara, and apart from his unsatisfactory school reports he gave me no cause for concern. It was not to be expected, though, that he would not sometimes get into mischief, especially when I was away, and one day he had amused himself tormenting the Vihara cat. For this Jivaka had chastised him with a slipper, a terrible indignity by local standards. Dupchen had been very angry, and he had threatened to knife his assailant. He would not have minded had Jivaka beaten him with his hand or even with a stick, he told me, for he knew he should not have tormented the cat; but the shame and humiliation of being beaten with a shoe was more than he could bear. I had therefore to explain to Jivaka what being struck with, or even touched by, another person's shoe meant in Indian (and Nepalese) culture, whereupon he apologized to

Dupchen and insisted on shaking hands with him to the accompaniment of 'No hard feelings, I hope.' I could see that Dupchen was puzzled by this strange public school ritual, but he shook hands nonetheless, and peace was restored to the Vihara.

The next time I went out on tour, I took the precaution of taking Jivaka with me as far as Sarnath, where I arranged for him to stay until my return, as I did not want to risk any further trouble between him and Dupchen. Sarnath was one of the four principal holy places, for it was here that the Buddha had set in motion the Wheel of the Dharma. Besides ancient monuments, it had temples and monasteries, and a small body of Theravadin monks who looked after the needs of the pilgrims, and I thought Jivaka would in any case benefit from a wider range of Buddhist contacts. From the letters beginning 'Dear Daddy' that followed me round central and western India I learned that he was helping out in the dispensary, that he had given nicknames to all the monks (my old friend Sangharatana was 'Sammy'), and that he was writing a book on Buddhism for children. On my returning to Sarnath, however, I received a shock. No sooner had I arrived than Jivaka took me aside and told me that the monks had agreed to his ordination as a samanera or novice provided I, too, agreed. The ceremony was to take place the following morning. This put me in a quandary. I did not want to disappoint Jivaka, but neither did I want to connive at the deception of my brother monks, the very thought of which was abhorrent to me. In the end, I decided to say nothing about Jivaka not being really a man. Strict rules governed ordination as a bhikkhu or monk proper, but in the case of samanera ordination a degree of irregularity was, I knew, permitted, or at least tolerated. There was also the fact that it would be difficult to veto Jivaka's ordination without giving a reason, especially as the other monks were all very much in favour of it. Such were the sophistries with which I sought to soothe my uneasy conscience.

The following morning I arrived at the Sinhalese Temple late, and took my seat at the back, behind the other monks. ──────

'Come and sit in the front,' the abbot called out to me. 'You're his teacher.'

In the front I therefore had to sit, though my heart was not in the proceedings, and afterwards my congratulations lacked warmth.

Jivaka failed to notice this. 'The next step is bhikkhu ordination,' he declared with evident satisfaction.

In normal circumstances, bhikkhu ordination would indeed have been the next step, but in Jivaka's case the circumstances were not normal. However, I did not remind him of this. Instead I simply asked him why he was so anxious to become a bhikkhu.

'It's because I want to be able to ordain my own disciples,' he replied unhesitatingly.

'But you won't be able to ordain others until you've been a bhikkhu for at least ten years,' I pointed out.

His face darkened. 'I'm not going to bother about a little thing like that,' he retorted.

'*Jivaka will have to be stopped,*' I said to myself, for it was obvious that the erstwhile disciple of Lobsang Rampa was dominated by spiritual ambition and that ordination was for him only a means to the attainment of essentially egoistic ends. By his own admission, he was a great believer in the fait accompli, and I now knew he did not scruple to act in accordance with that belief. He had caught me out once, but he would not catch me out a second time.

Thus resolving, I left for Kalimpong. I cannot be certain whether Jivaka accompanied me and returned to Sarnath later, or whether he stayed behind and never saw Kalimpong again. Whichever it was, he was certainly in Sarnath by the summer of 1959, a year after his arrival at the Vihara, and letters beginning 'Dear Daddy' were again pouring from his prolific pen. They were often full of complaints, as well as requests. One of his biggest complaints was about the amount of money he had to spend on postage stamps, for he appeared to be carrying on an extensive correspondence with various editors and publishers. The letters were suspiciously silent on the subject of bhikkhu ordination. One day, however, I heard on the monastic grapevine that he had asked the Sarnath monks to allow him to take the 'next step'. Evidently another fait accompli was being planned for my benefit. I therefore at once wrote officially to the abbot and his brother monks, informing them that Jivaka was a transsexual, apologizing for having not informed them before, and leaving it to them, in their wisdom, to decide whether or not he qualified for ordination as a bhikkhu. This was towards the end of 1959.

Jivaka was furious. In a bitter, angry letter he accused me of betraying secrets confided to me 'under the seal of the confessional'. He seemed to be rather fond of the phrase, for he used it more than once in the letter, as well as subsequently. I replied that I was not a Roman Catholic priest and that there was no question of any 'confessional'. Nonetheless I had kept his secret faithfully, even to the extent of keeping silent about it so that he could be ordained as a samanera, despite my misgivings. But bhikkhu ordination was an entirely different matter, and now that he had asked for it, as I had heard, I could no longer remain silent. I was his friend, and I wished him well, but my loyalty to the Order of Bhikkhus, as represented by Sangharatana and the other Sarnath monks, took precedence of my loyalty to him. Jivaka was unable to accept this, as was obvious from his reply. In his view, my loyalty to him took precedence over all other loyalties, so that in revealing his secret to my fellow bhikkhus in Sarnath I had been guilty of a shameful betrayal for which there could be no forgiveness. Though he did not compare me to Judas Iscariot, the tone of his letter suggested that this was the kind of light in which he now saw me. Thus from being good, kind Daddy I became, almost overnight, the wicked, cruel stepfather who had unaccountably prevented poor little Jivaka from getting something he badly wanted.

All the same, he continued writing to me. He wrote less frequently than before, and his letters now began 'Dear Sangharakshita'. A few weeks after the 'betrayal' he assured me he was not angry, and that his faith in human nature had long been weak. Most of his letters contained the familiar complaints, and in some of them he was sarcastic at my expense. In the articles he published, and in the correspondence columns of the English-language press, he made a point of disagreeing with me, or criticizing me, whenever he could. Perhaps this was an example of what I was to term, years later, 'delayed adolescent rebellion'. In one of his letters he assured me that in not becoming his guru I had missed a wonderful opportunity. In another he ascribed my treatment of him to jealousy. I was jealous of him, he claimed, because he came from an aristocratic family (which he did), because he was better educated (which he was), and because he was spiritually more advanced (which was at least debatable), and I wanted to hold him back lest, endowed as he was with these advantages, he should become better known than myself as a Buddhist writer and teacher.

During the three years that followed, Jivaka left the Theravada for the Mahayana form of Buddhism, was re-ordained as a Tibetan *getsul* or novice, took the name of Lobzang (sic) Jivaka, and wrote a popular abridgement of Dr W.Y. Evans-Wentz's *Tibet's Great Yogi, Milarepa*, which was published by Murray in the well-known Wisdom of the East series. In 1960 he spent three months in a Gelug monastery in Ladakh, in the western Himalayas. Unfortunately, he was refused permission to re-enter Ladakh which was in a prohibited area, and reluctantly returned to Sarnath.

In the spring of 1962 I received a review copy of *Imji Getsul: an English Buddhist in a Tibetan Monastery*. It was not *Out of the Ordinary*, as I had at first thought. Neither was it, apparently, one of the three versions of his autobiography which, Jivaka had told me, he had recently prepared for publication. One version showed me in a favourable light, one in a very unfavourable light, and one in a light that was neither favourable nor unfavourable. Which version was published, he informed me, would depend on whether or not I cooperated with him. What this 'cooperation' meant he did not say, but I assumed it had something to do with the higher monastic ordination, which I knew him to be still desperately seeking.

Imji Getsul, it turned out, was mainly a quite interesting account of the three months Jivaka had spent at Rizong Gompa. There was even a photograph of him with some of the other monks, looking not very happy. But there was no mention of the sex change, nor of Lobsang Rampa, nor of the Secret Order of the Potala, nor of his wanting to acquire psychic powers. Since there was no mention of the sex change there could be no truthful account of the circumstances which had brought him, eventually, to Kalimpong, nor of how he had come to be called Jivaka. I appeared briefly in the book simply as 'the English bhikkhu in Kalimpong', my name not being given, and his account of me could be said to fall into the 'not very favourable' category. I had taught him nothing, had not allowed him to read any books from my library except those I selected, and had made him work all day. 'What was behind this policy I never discovered,' he wrote in an evident plea for the reader's pity.

I at once wrote to Jivaka, reproaching him for his ingratitude and reminding him of some of the things I had taught him. Nor did I fail to mention that it was I who had opened his eyes to the fact that Lobsang Rampa was not a genuine Tibetan lama and that the Secret Order of the Potala was no more than a product of the latter's fertile imagination. Whether Jivaka ever received my letter I do not know. On 15 May he died at the Civil Hospital, Dalhousie (Punjab), after less than two days of illness, and his body was immediately cremated. No one knew why he was in Dalhousie, and the cause of his death remained a mystery.

Chapter Six

FAMILY FORTUNES

THERE ARE PEOPLE who insert themselves into our lives by imperceptible degrees, and whom we can remember knowing without being able to recall when we first met them. Such a one was Rigdzing Wangpo, a Lhasa-born Tibetan who lived up at Tirpai in a wooden bungalow not far from the residence of Gergen Tharchin, the proprietor of the Tibet Mirror Press and editor of the *Tibet Mirror*, whose first wife was Rigdzing Wangpo's sister. Though I knew him for seven years or more, he seemed not to change during that period but to have remained the same thin, 45-year-old man with a long, lean face deeply furrowed down both sides, an amused expression, and a huge carbuncle on his left cheek. As a young man he had studied Pali in Ceylon, besides working for two years at the School of Oriental Languages in London, and Tibetan friends told me he was a fine poet and writer in his native tongue. By his own admission, he was something of a womanizer, and well-acquainted with the pleasures and pains of love. Recently, however, he had resolved to lead a more regular life, married a young Tibetan girl, and settled down with her in the wooden bungalow. A daughter was soon born to them, but when the child was a few months old, the young mother, who was only seventeen and rather wild, suddenly walked out on Rigdzing Wangpo, taking the baby with her.

This gave Rigdzing Wangpo food for serious thought, and he eventually concluded that the time had come for him to renounce the world and its false delights. He therefore asked me to ordain him as a Theravadin samanera, for by this time we were well acquainted. At first I refused point-blank, for I thought it would be inappropriate for me to be in a formal guru-disciple relationship with someone so much older than myself. Moreover, Rigdzing Wangpo was a Tibetan, and it seemed strange that he should not want to be ordained within the Tibetan monastic tradition, especially as he was on friendly terms with Dhardo Rimpoche and did, I knew, respect him highly. Naturally I explained my position to him, but the would-be samanera remained politely adamant. He wanted to be ordained, and he wanted to be ordained by nobody but me. In the end I relented, especially as it had become clear that although he was not openly critical of Tibetan Buddhism, he had serious reservations about some aspects of it and definitely wished to be ordained within the Theravadin monastic tradition. He was ordained on 20 July 1958, in the shrine-room of the Vihara, and I gave him the name Prajnaloka or 'Light of Wisdom'. For a few months all was well. The new samanera occupied himself with teaching and translation work, dividing his time between the Vihara and his bungalow at Tirpai, but spending most of it at the Vihara. Then one day, when he was at the bungalow, his truant wife unexpectedly appeared with the baby. She did not want the bother of looking after it any longer, she declared. He was the father, and now *he* would have to look after it. Whereupon she left, leaving the baby with Prajnaloka. It all happened so quickly that Prajnaloka, who at the best of times was slow of speech, had no time to say anything. He could only sit staring through the open door at the retreating form of the young woman, trying to grasp what had happened to him. Here he was, newly ordained, but now with a young child to care for and bring up!

Once he had got over the initial shock, Prajnaloka accepted the situation philosophically. No doubt he was experiencing the fruit of the bad karma he had created by his affairs with women, he told me with a rueful smile the next time we met. A similar reflection may well have occurred to a Newar samanera who appeared in Kalimpong around this time and who soon found himself in a predicament not unlike Prajnaloka's.

Ananda was about the same age as myself, but shorter, plumper, and, like many Newars, very fair-skinned. Though I have referred to him as a samanera I am not sure if he really was one. He certainly wore a yellow robe, as did his two wives, who apparently had 'gone forth' from home into the homeless life when he did. All three were shaven-headed. On their arrival in Kalimpong the little group did not receive a very warm welcome from their Newar co-religionists, some of whom jeered at Ananda, saying that one who, as a layman, was so lustful that he needed two wives, could hardly be expected to make a success of the religious life. Ananda bore their scoffs and jeers patiently, as did the two women, and I more than once saw the three of them quietly going for alms in the bazaar, as I myself had once done.

One day he came to see me. He came alone, and as the visit was repeated a number of times during the next few weeks I quickly got to know him quite well. He was an enthusiastic meditator, with some experience of higher meditative states. Meditation seemed, in fact, to be the only aspect of the Dharma in which he was interested. Before long he was urging me to accompany him into the forest. We would stay there together, devoting all our time to meditation. (He did not say what his two women would be doing while we were thus engaged.) But I was not convinced that the forest would provide me with better conditions for meditation than did the Vihara; in any case, I did not yet feel ready to be a full-time meditator. Ananda did, however, persuade me to take up a special form of *anapana-sati* or 'respiration mindfulness', with the traditional form of which I had long been familiar. I had practised the new form for only a few minutes when I experienced a sudden upsurge of *priti* or 'rapture' so unbearably intense that it almost knocked me from my seat and left me gasping for breath. Shortly after this experience of mine, one of Ananda's wives gave birth to a child, which was soon to be seen wrapped in a piece of yellow cloth. I did not know when the three had 'gone forth', and it was possible that the woman was pregnant at that time. The other Newar Buddhists took a less charitable view. Ananda was heaped with abuse for having broken his vows, and life was made so difficult for them that in the end the little group of wanderers left Kalimpong. I never heard of Ananda again, though I made enquiries after him for several years.

Unlike Ananda, Prajnaloka did not have to leave Kalimpong. There was some amusement at the way karma had caught up with him, but he had broken no vows, and most of those who knew him could not but feel sympathy for a man who, no longer young, and only recently ordained, had been unexpectedly saddled with the responsibility of single-handedly bringing up a child. Not that this new responsibility changed Prajnaloka's way of life completely. He continued to be based at Tirpai, continued to teach his students, continued to wear the yellow robe with which he had been invested only a few months earlier, and greeted friends he passed in the street with the same amused smile. Only in one particular was there a change in his outward aspect: the disfiguring carbuncle had disappeared. It disappeared either just before or just after his ordination, but in any case during the time Jivaka was with us, for it was Jivaka who had performed the operation. I might well have forgotten the incident, had I not learned from it something about myself. We had laid Prajnaloka out on the dining-room table, and having given him a local anaesthetic Jivaka was hacking away at the carbuncle with a razor blade while I caught the blood in a basin. There was a lot of blood. I experienced no conscious revulsion at the sight, but my stomach seemed to turn a somersault, and I had to rush to the bathroom and vomit, returning a minute later to hold the basin again. Thus I learned that my stomach had a life, even a mind, of its own, and that I had no more control over it than I had over my heart or my lungs. When Jivaka had stitched up the wound with an ordinary needle and thread, Prajnaloka sat up and asked to see the carbuncle. Jivaka gave it to him, whereupon he held it in the palm of his hand, studied it carefully for a while, and at length took it away with him. In a few weeks the wound had healed and there was no scar.

Prajnaloka not only kept the carbuncle but showed it to his friends and related to them the whole story of the operation. In his unhurried, deliberate way he was an excellent raconteur, with a sly sense of humour, and people enjoyed listening to him no less than he enjoyed entertaining and instructing them with his anecdotes and reminiscences. His favourite theme, especially after his wife deserted him, was the fickle, vain, unreliable, deceitful, treacherous, superficial, manipulative, and generally unsatisfactory nature of the female sex. This was also the subject of a long poem he was writing in classical Tibetan, verses from which he would sometimes read aloud for the benefit of those who understood Tibetan and translate for the benefit of those who did not. It was not that Prajnaloka was a misogynist, of course. He was simply giving expression to the traditional monastic view of women, especially as illustrated by his own experience over the years. Besides having a favourite theme, he had a favourite audience. This consisted of the young men, both Nepalese and Tibetan, who came to the Vihara from time to time, whether to see me or to take part in our regular full-moon-day pujas. Some were former students of mine, others the sons and nephews of people I knew. Among these young men were Durgaprasad and Budhkumar, two friends of about the same age who often came to the Vihara together. Like the others, they listened to Prajnaloka's anecdotes and admonitions with great interest, but in the case of one of them, at least, they did not benefit from what they heard as much as they could have done.

I had known Durga, as he was generally called, since he was fifteen, when he accompanied an older cousin who was studying with me to the semi-derelict wooden bungalow in which I was then living. He was somewhat below average height, tended to be un-communicative, and from beneath drooping eyelids surveyed the world with a lazy, contemplative gaze. His father, Setu Singh, who was the Kalimpong municipality's head fitter, was well known to me. An active, gnome-like little man in traditional Nepalese dress, complete with black pillbox, he had a weather-beaten face, a worried expression, and a big nose – a nose that Durga, unlike his brothers, had inherited. Whenever we met, which was usually when he came to read the Vihara's water meter (we had mains water but no electricity), Setu Singh would complain to me in an injured tone about his son, whom he always referred to as 'Mr Durga'. His complaint was to the effect that Durga was lazy, neglected his studies, spent too much time roaming the bazaar, and disregarded his father's wishes. In all this there was a good deal of truth, as I well knew; but there was another side to the story, as I also knew.

Nepalese fathers believed in being strict with their sons, even to the point of harshness, and were convinced that such treatment was in their sons' best interests. As a result, there was often little confidence between father and son, and little communication. Durga, I knew, avoided his father as much as he could, and if he wanted to ask him something he did so through his mother, a pious Hindu lady who occasionally came to the Vihara to see me and to pay her respects to the Buddha. Yet Setu Singh was a kindly, helpful man who loved his unsatisfactory son and could be hurt by the latter's avoidance of him, even though that avoidance was the result of his own treatment of him. When Ronald Boughen invited Durga to spend a week with him in Delhi (this was before Ronald's migration to the Kulu Valley) he said nothing to his father about the trip. His father knew he was going, however, and on the morning of his departure tucked a five rupee note into the breast pocket of his jacket, with the intention of giving it to Durga when he came to say goodbye. But Durga never came. The disappointment must have rankled, for the next time we met, Setu Singh told me about the incident with evident emotion.

While it was true that Durga spent too much time roaming the bazaar, as his father believed, it was no less true that he probably spent too much time at the bungalow where the older cousin through whom he had met me lived with his parents, younger brother, and three sisters. The family was well known in the town, the father being the popular 'Nepali doctor' at the Scottish Mission Hospital as well as the subdivisional civil surgeon. All five children were strikingly good-looking, had many friends, and readily took part in such social life as was available to the Westernized younger generation. Old-fashioned members of the community to which the family belonged were of the opinion that their parents allowed the three girls far too much freedom, and they were therefore not at all surprised when Meera, the youngest of the three, was found to be pregnant. I had known Meera for as long as I had known Durga. When she was twelve or thirteen her parents asked me to give her practice in English conversation whenever I happened to be at their place. She seemed to enjoy her lessons with me, but she was far from being as bright as she was pretty, and did not profit from them very much. I noticed, however, that she was always eager for news of Durga who, she knew, sometimes visited me, and did not hesitate to question me about what he had been doing. As she was so young, I naturally thought that she had no more than a cousinly interest in him. Yet she must have conceived a definite liking for him even then. That liking must have persisted and grown stronger with the passing of time, and eventually, four or five years later, must have been actively reciprocated, for it was Durga who was responsible for Meera's present condition.

The culprit was severely criticized by both the extended families involved. It was not simply that he had seduced an unmarried girl. Though he and Meera were not first cousins, and though in their community the rules governing such matters were less strict than they were in the higher castes, the two were near enough in blood for their conduct to be regarded as scandalous.

But Durga was unrepentant. 'They know what young men are like,' he grumbled to me. 'If they don't want their daughters to get pregnant they should keep them locked up.'

It was much too late for anyone to think of locking Meera up now that she was pregnant, but it was not too late for her to be rehabilitated, at least to an extent. Rehabilitation meant getting her married to Durga before the child was born. The elders of the two families therefore agreed that on a certain day Durga should go to the house where Meera's mother now lived with her daughters and then, when it was dark, take Meera by the hand, so to speak, and conduct her to her new home under his parents' roof. Meera's mother, however, was adamant that they should be escorted by a responsible elder, for she was convinced that otherwise Durga would throw her daughter into a ditch at the first opportunity and run away. Nor was this all. Since Meera's father had recently died, and since her elder brother was working in Calcutta, she was insistent that I should be that responsible elder and make sure that Meera arrived safely at her destination. I did not want to take on this responsibility, which was more suited to a layman than a monk, but in the end I agreed to do so, for I was fond of Meera, and though I knew she was in no danger of being thrown into a ditch, I also knew that Durga did not really want to marry her and probably would not be a very agreeable companion that evening.

There was no moon when the three of us set out, and it was quite dark. We walked up to the T-junction where the High Street began, and from there down the winding hillside road that led, eventually, to Teesta Bridge. It was not long before Durga, without saying a word, detached himself from Meera and me and walked on ahead as though he had nothing to do with us, from time to time disappearing round a bend in the road. Meera was evidently pleased with how things were turning out for her, and chattered gaily all the way. After walking for nearly an hour we left the road and with some difficulty made our way down the terraced hillside that fell away to the right, Durga all the while keeping well ahead. Ten minutes later we saw a shadowy form disappear into a no less shadowy cottage, and shortly afterwards we were inside it ourselves. There was no sign of Durga. Someone lit a kerosene lamp, and Durga's two sisters called Meera to their room, where the three of them could be heard talking and laughing. Presently Durga's parents appeared. Both were in a sombre mood, and little was said. When I had drunk a cup of tea Setu Singh called Durga and rather sharply ordered him to see me up the road. In little more than an hour I was back at the Vihara.

A month or so later, Durga and Meera were married. The wedding was a very modest affair, I was told, with only close relations and a few friends attending. When her time came, Meera returned to her mother's house for the delivery, as the custom was, but the child was stillborn, and Durga and Meera gradually drifted apart.

Though Durga was averse to marriage, he had no objection to his friends getting married, and was even prepared to help them in this connection. He was certainly prepared to help Budhkumar elope with the girl he wished to marry, despite the fact that both his own parents and the girl's were absolutely opposed to the match. I had known Budhkumar as long as I had known Durga, but until recently we had met only intermittently, as he was usually at college down in the plains, studying civil engineering. He was a cheerful, good-natured extrovert, who was interested in body-building and would confess, laughingly, to being a victim of a bad habit of chewing tobacco. Quite early in our friendship he confided to me that he was in love with a beautiful, modest, well-behaved girl who belonged, as he did, to the Hindu Newar caste. In their caste, however, marriage was strictly prohibited between those having a common ancestor up to seven generations back. He and Radha were related in the fifth degree, that is to say, they had a common ancestor five generations back, so the future seemed dark. I did my best to cheer him up, which was not difficult, and the following day I addressed to him a sonnet beginning,

> Your sorrow is my sorrow, friend, and so
> When yesterday I saw you, wan with grief,
> I yearned to give some comfort or relief,

And thus it was, the reason of your woe,
Not merely curiously, I sought to know.

The poem concluded with a reference to the rainbow that had
appeared in the sky as we were talking, and which I saw as a symbol
of hope. Nonetheless, as the prospect of his marrying Radha was so
remote, I asked Budhkumar one day why he did not marry the older
of Meera's two elder sisters, with whom, as I knew, he had long had
an illicit relationship.

He was quite shocked. 'Oh, I wouldn't want to marry a girl of bad
character!' he exclaimed.

Radha was not kept locked up, as Durga believed daughters ought
to be, but her parents made quite sure that she and Budhkumar
never had an opportunity to meet. The most they could hope for was
a distant glimpse of each other on the occasion of some big family
gathering such as – ironically – a wedding. But love will find a way,
and Budhkumar had for some time been carrying on a clandestine
correspondence with Radha through the agency of a small boy
whom he bribed to smuggle letters to her and bring back her replies,
and it was in the course of this correspondence that the elopement
had been discussed, agreed upon, and planned. The plan was
simple. The house in which Radha lived with her parents and other
members of the family was situated on the other side of town, a mile
or more beyond the Old Bhutan Palace. This house had a garden,
and between the garden and the road there was a hedge, and in the
hedge, not too near the house, there was a gap. At two o'clock in the
morning, on a certain moonless night, Radha would tell the aunt or
sister who slept with her that she needed to visit the toilet, which
was an outside one, and located a few yards from the gap in the
hedge. Budhkumar and Durga would be waiting for her with a jeep
on the other side of the gap. She had only to squeeze through it, and
they would be off.

The two friends spent the earlier part of the night at the Vihara,
leaving at 1.30 for their rendezvous with Radha. Budhkumar was
excited and anxious, Durga a little more communicative than usual.

In the morning I received a visit from Budhkumar's father, a
choleric old gentleman whom I had once met at his own place. He
came accompanied by his youngest son, who was in Budhkumar's
confidence and who evidently was saying nothing. I was unable to

tell my visitor where his son was, for I did not know. He must have suspected I was keeping something back, for he did not leave without remarking that it was common knowledge Budhkumar did nothing without consulting me. Two days later Durga came to see me. Things had gone according to plan, he reported, and Budhkumar and Radha were now staying in the Duars. Later I heard that they were married and living in Gangtok, where Budhkumar was working as a civil engineer. In due course a child was born, whereupon intermediaries set to work, and a reconciliation between Budhkumar and his family was arranged. He and Radha fell at his parents' feet and begged their forgiveness. Tears were shed all round, and the two old people had the satisfaction of seeing their first grandchild.

Chapter Seven

POETRY AND PROSE

ALTHOUGH I WAS LIVING on the outskirts of a small town in the foot-hills of the eastern Himalayas, I experienced no sense of isolation from the wider world. As Avalokiteshvara, the Bodhisattva of compassion, in the form of a cuckoo, tells the other birds in James H. Cousins' *A Tibetan Banner*, written many years earlier while the Irish poet was visiting Kalimpong,

> Who seeks the world, his heart beclouds
> In the thick solitude of crowds;
> But he who seeks a peak apart
> Must hold the world within his heart.

That I experienced no sense of isolation from that wider world, and at times could even hold it within my heart to an extent, was due largely to my being in correspondence with fellow Buddhists in the West, in South-East Asia, and in other parts of India, some of whom wrote to me regularly and at great length. Particularly when I was not on tour, a good deal of my time was therefore spent replying to letters, for I enjoyed replying to them almost as much as I enjoyed receiving them. Some letters gave news of Buddhist activities in London, or Paris, or Budapest, while others invited me to speak at this or that inter-religious conference, or put questions about the Buddha's teaching, or asked me to accept the writer as a disciple. Regardless of whether or not I was on tour, there was always the next issue of the Buddhist monthly journal to be brought out, which meant selecting and arranging the articles I had received, finding fillers and illustrations, and writing my editorial for the month.

These editorials dealt with a variety of topics and were unsigned. In 'The Buddhist World' (October 1959) I argued that a Buddhist should be acquainted with all forms of Buddhism; in 'Spreading the Dharma' (January 1959) I urged lazy Buddhists to bestir themselves, and in 'A Serious Matter' (August 1961) I deplored the practice of ordaining samaneras but not teaching them anything, for unless it was abandoned 'we may have people in yellow robes but we shall not have a Sangha'. Some editorials were concerned with what was happening in this or that Buddhist country. 'Stop the Rot' (August 1960), written in the wake of the assassination of the prime minister of Ceylon by a Buddhist monk, called upon the new government to take the management of ecclesiastical properties out of the hands of the monks, while 'A Disturbing Dispute' (March–April 1961) commented on the differences that had arisen in Korea between the celibate bhikkhus and those who, during the Japanese occupation, had become Japanese-style married priests. I occasionally allowed myself to be a little controversial, even polemical, as I did in 'Religion vs God' (June 1960) and in 'Stars and Stupidity' (February 1962), the 'stupidity' being that of the millions of Hindus who were engaged, that month, in burning food-offerings in the sacred fire and feeding brahmins in order to avert the terrible disasters predicted by the astrologers.

There were also months when I drew the attention of the authorities to the way in which certain ancient Buddhist sites were being vandalized. In 'More Vandalism' (June 1961), for example, I complained that at Karle a Hindu temple had been erected immediately in front of the entrance to the main Chaitya Cave, the largest and most magnificent of its kind in India. What was more, the deity installed in the temple was a blood-thirsty local goddess to whom fowls and goats were regularly sacrificed, being slaughtered *within the protected area of the cave itself.*

From time to time I struck a more reflective note, as in 'Rainy Season Retreat' (August 1958), in 'Meditation on a Flame' (October 1958), and in 'Words and Meaning' (September 1958), in which I observed, 'Much unnecessary dust has been raised by people, not excluding experienced scholars, confidently writing and speaking about Buddhism without first ascertaining what its main keywords are and what are their respective meanings.'

The ascertaining of these keywords and their meanings was one of the things I had tried to do in *A Survey of Buddhism*, published in 1957, and which I also tried to do, on a smaller scale, in the second and third of the three books I wrote, or began to write, during my time at the Vihara. The first was *The Rainbow Road: From Tooting Broadway to Kalimpong*, on which I started when Jivaka was staying with us. He had just finished writing his own autobiography, *Out of the Ordinary*, and one day he asked me why I did not write *mine*.

'But what would be the point?' I protested, 'I haven't had nearly such an interesting life as you. In fact, my life has been quite ordinary, and even if I did manage to write my autobiography who on earth would want to read it?'

'Nonsense!' retorted Jivaka, in his usual brusque fashion, 'You've had a *very* interesting life, and if you were to write your autobiography a lot of people would want to read it. It might even become a best-seller.'

I remained unconvinced. I had suggested that Jivaka should write his autobiography because there were, I suspected, things he needed to get off his chest, and writing his autobiography seemed a good way for him to do this. In my own case no such consideration applied. There was nothing of a personal nature of which I particularly wanted to disburden myself. However, Jivaka returned to the attack, pointing out that I wasn't very busy just then, and the following morning I sat down at my desk and cast my mind back to far-away Tooting.

I wrote rapidly, as the memories came to me, without giving much thought to the arrangement of my material, and with little regard for literary style. Each morning I handed over to Jivaka what I had written the previous day, and he typed it for me, a service he rendered for as long as he remained at the Vihara, after which I had to do my own typing. In his usual high-handed fashion, he did not hesitate to edit my work as he thought fit. He particularly objected to what he called my book lists, by which he meant my detailed account of my early reading, and cut them ruthlessly. This did not bother me, as at this stage I had no thought of publication, and I continued to write for the sheer joy of writing. Since I had no old letters or diaries to help me, I had to rely entirely on my memory. What I was writing was therefore not my autobiography, in the sense of a complete, well-documented account of the events and circumstances of my life so far, but simply my *memoirs*. Thus I remembered, and wrote about, my childhood in Tooting, about my confinement to bed for two years with supposed heart disease, about my indebtedness to the *Children's Encyclopaedia*, about my involvement with the Boys' Brigade, about the Blitz and my evacuation to Devon with my school, about the break-up of my parents' marriage, about the two years I spent working for the London County Council, about my realization that I was a Buddhist and had always been one, about my four years in the Army, which took me to India, Ceylon, and Singapore, about my leaving the Army and teaming up in India with a Bengali friend, about our encounter with Anandamayi and her fractious disciples, about our 'going forth' together as freelance wandering ascetics, and about the multiple rainbows that spanned the road as, shaven-headed and clad in our new saffron robes, we walked from the Punjab hills down to the plains.

As I wrote, I was astonished how much I remembered. It was as though I had in front of me a huge library or archive of materials and had only to reach out and take down the next volume. Thus it was not surprising that within two years of my starting work on *The Rainbow Road* I should have produced well over a 100,000 words. Not that the production of those words had proceeded without interruption. During the same period I undertook a number of extensive preaching tours in the plains, some of which kept me away from Kalimpong for months together. Then in 1962 I received an invitation to contribute the articles on Buddhism to the *Oriya Encyclopaedia* and put the memoirs aside in order to concentrate on the new assignment. I was sorry to put them aside, for in the process of working on them I was learning a lot about the art and craft of writing; but I thought it better to spend my time making the Dharma available to Oriya-speaking people than to spend it writing about myself.

The *Oriya Encyclopaedia* was one of the fourteen regional language encyclopaedias then being sponsored by the Government of India, and the invitation to write the articles on Buddhism came from the Oriya poet and dramatist Mandhar Mansinha, who was already known to me. I had met him in Sambalpur, a town in the state of Orissa. He took the chair when I gave a lecture at the local college, of which he was principal, and we had remained in touch ever since. In inviting me to write the articles, Dr Mansinha had left me free to treat the great subject in my own way, and I therefore set to work with a will. I began by writing the articles on the Buddha, the Dharma, and the Sangha respectively, then went on to write those on the scriptures of Buddhism, and on its numerous sects and schools. As with *The Rainbow Road*, in the course of two years I produced well over 100,000 words, despite the usual interruptions. This was far in excess of what was wanted, and only a few of the articles I had written were, therefore, translated into Oriya and included in the encyclopaedia. As it was, by allotting to Buddhism even as much space as this, Dr Mansinha incurred orthodox Hindu wrath, and eventually resigned his position as editor-in-chief.

Though only a few of the articles I had written found a place in the *Oriya Encyclopaedia*, I did not think the time I had spent on the assignment wasted. As I quickly realized, the thirty-nine articles I had produced fell quite naturally into three groups. The first group consisted of the articles on the Buddha, the Dharma, and the Sangha, and these went to form Parts I, II, and III of *The Three Jewels: An Introduction to Buddhism*, published in 1967. The Three Jewels were the triple embodiment of an ideal, and it was commitment to the realization of that ideal by following a certain way of life in the company of others similarly committed that made one a Buddhist. This was what was traditionally known as 'Going for Refuge' to the Three Jewels, which, as I wrote in the preface to the volume, was 'an act which, though it may find ceremonial expression, is essentially a profound inner experience, a spiritual rebirth or "conversion", as a result of which one's whole life is transformed and re-oriented.' The second group of articles consisted of those on the Buddhist scriptures, from the Monastic Code to the Tantras, preceded by those on Buddhism and Language and on The Oral Tradition. These articles went to make up *The Eternal Legacy: An Introduction to the Canonical Literature of Buddhism*, published in 1985.

The third group of articles, and by far the smallest, consisted of the three I had written on the sects and schools of Buddhism. There were to have been many more, but I never got round to writing them, mainly because I had been invited by the Oxford University Press to write the article on Buddhism for their new edition of *The Legacy of India*, an assignment I managed to complete before leaving for England in August 1964. The articles making up the third group, both written and unwritten, were provisionally entitled 'The Pattern of Development in Buddhism'. According to the first article in this group, that pattern would be revealed if certain principles of classification were to be systematically applied to the different Buddhist traditions. There were seven such principles, each of which I discussed briefly. They were: (1) geographical provenance, (2) *yana* membership, (3) spiritual faculty (*indriya*) emphasized, (4) principal Buddha-form revered, (5) canonical basis, (6) doctrinal position, and (7) line of transmission from master to disciple. Thus the Nyingma school, for example, would be described as a Tibetan form of Vajrayana which emphasizes meditation, revered Samantabhadra as principal Buddha-form, had its canonical basis in the Nyingma Tantras and the *Rinchen Terdzen*, taught Atiyoga doctrine, and traced its line of transmission back to the three men of Kham (the so-called Lower Vinaya) in respect of *upasampada* or bhikshu ordination, to Nagarjuna and Shantideva in respect of Bodhisattva ordination (*samvara*), and to Padmasambhava in respect of *abhisheka* or Tantric initiation.

The remaining articles in the third group were not the only ones I did not get round to writing. I had also planned to write articles on meditation in the three *yanas*, and on forms and functions of Buddhist art. Together with *The Three Jewels* and *The Eternal Legacy*, and the completed 'Pattern of Development in Buddhism', they would, I hoped, eventually make up a series of five independent volumes under the general title of 'The Heritage of Buddhism'. But alas for the aspirations and ambitions of men! Events and circumstances prevented me from finishing the third volume and from even starting on the fourth and fifth. For me, as for Abt Vogler, it was a case of 'On the earth the broken arcs; in the heaven, a perfect round.'

The writing of *The Three Jewels* and *The Eternal Legacy* involved a good deal of reading and re-reading, both of the canonical texts and of modern scholarly works. This was particularly so in the case of *The Eternal Legacy*. Reading and writing about the Agamas/Nikayas and the great Mahayana sutras I felt myself transported to another world. It was not always the same world. At one time it might be the world of ancient India, a world of green paddy fields, of vast, dark forests, of little groups of thatched mud-walled huts, of women walking to the well with earthenware pots balanced on their heads – a world of farmers and artisans, brahmins and wandering ascetics, merchants and princes. It was the world in which the Buddha had lived and taught twenty-five centuries ago, now in a village moot hall, now beneath the spreading branches of a banyan tree, now to invisible presences in the silence of the night. I had visited some of the places where the Buddha had taught, and it was therefore not difficult for me to imagine what they looked like in his day. Nor was it difficult for me even to imagine what the Buddha himself looked like, at least to the outward eye. I did not see him as he was depicted in the popular religious art of South-East Asia and India, where he appeared looking like a modern Theravadin bhikkhu – well groomed, clad in brand-new yellow robes, and carrying an embroidered shoulder bag. I saw him, instead, as a man who looked much more like some of the Hindu sadhus I had encountered during my wandering days – unshaven, clad in ragged, dust-stained garments, and with few or no possessions. It was therefore small wonder that – as the texts I was reading attested – people sometimes failed to realize that this man was none other than the Buddha, the Enlightened One.

At another time I might be transported not to the world of ancient India and the human, historical Shakyamuni, but to an archetypal world inhabited by innumerable Buddhas and Bodhisattvas and resounding with the sublime tones of the Dharma. Or I might be transported to a transfigured Vulture Peak, where a transfigured Shakyamuni relates for the benefit of the assembled Bodhisattvas, Arahants, divinities of various orders, and human beings a series of magnificent parables, and where various wonders take place. Then again, I might find myself in the legendary world of Lanka and the ten-headed Ravana, lord of the demons, and there hear the Buddha discoursing to Mahamati, the great Bodhisattva, on the self-realization of Noble Wisdom (*aryajnana*), the Store-consciousness (*alayavijnana*), and Mind-only (*cittamatra*), and on many other subtle and abstruse aspects of the Dharma.

From the world, or worlds, of the great Mahayana sutras in particular, I would not always find it easy to turn my attention to a world in which one had to keep accounts and pay bills, even for a Vihara. Sometimes a good book would help me to make the transition. One such book had been given me by a European friend in Bombay.

'You'll like this book,' he told me, with a smile, 'It's just like a Mahayana sutra.'

The book was Olaf Stapledon's *Star Maker*. I did like it, and despite the absence of Buddhas and Bodhisattvas it really was like a Mahayana sutra. This could not be said of any of the other books I was reading at this time, though all of them contained elements of insight and imagination that were not incompatible with the spirit of the Dharma. Most of them had been given me by friends, and they included such classics of Western literature as *Don Quixote*, *The Faerie Queene*, the Poetical Works of Robert Burns, Eckermann's *Conversations with Goethe*, *Hard Times*, *The History of Henry Esmond*, and *Anna Karenina*. They all made a strong impression on me, in their different ways, and some of them remained favourites for the rest of my life. To me, it was not strange that I should read the classics of Western literature as well as the Buddhist scriptures, though my more austere Theravadin colleagues in Calcutta and Sarnath might raise their eyebrows to see me with a volume of English poetry in my hand. Both were necessary to me and I saw no reason why I should have to choose between them, as some people thought I should.

Ten years earlier, when I was staying at Buddha Kuti with Jagdish Kashyap, I had once received, by the same post, letters from two such people, one of them a Buddhist monk, the other a Buddhist laywoman. Both must have been reading my latest contributions to the Buddhist magazines of Ceylon. When I could write such excellent articles on Buddhist philosophy, the monk demanded, why did I waste my time writing those foolish poems? The laywoman took exactly the opposite view. When I could write such beautiful poems on Buddhism, she asked, why did I spend so much time writing those dry, intellectual articles? I agreed – and disagreed – with them both. The conflict was not so much between the philosophically-inclined monk and the poetry-loving laywoman as between the two sides of my own nature, the monastic-intellectual and the poetic-emotional, which I had not yet succeeded in reconciling and harmonizing. It was not until some time later, during my early years in Kalimpong, that I began to see not only the possibility of reconciliation and harmonization but also that the dichotomy on which the conflict was based was not so real as I had supposed.

I happened to be explaining Shelley's 'The Cloud' to three or four students who were preparing for the Intermediate Arts examination. They were all very attentive, there was a good rapport between us, and I found I was able to go more and more deeply into the meaning of the poem. The more deeply I went into it, the profounder and more universal that meaning seemed to be. After a while, as I plumbed depth upon depth of significance, the thought suddenly struck me that I was not simply elucidating Shelley's poem: *I was teaching the Dharma*. It was not that I was using the poem as a hook on which to hang an exposition of the Dharma. I had given myself to the poem; I had plunged into it as into an ocean, and the ocean had yielded up the pearl of the Dharma, a pearl that was already there, hidden in the depths, only waiting to be discovered. However, it was because I was already acquainted with the Dharma that I was able to recognize it when I encountered it in the poem. Indeed, if one was acquainted with the Dharma, and looked deeply enough, one could encounter the Dharma not just in Shelley's poem but also in other works of Western literature as well, perhaps, in painting and sculpture, and even in musical compositions. Not that one should go looking for the Dharma in any of them in a self-conscious and deliberate manner. One should simply give oneself to the poem, or painting, or song, and forget about the Dharma for the time being.

It was during my early years in Kalimpong, too, that I produced two essays in which I sought to determine the nature of the relation between religion and art and, in particular, between Buddhism and art. The two essays were 'The Meaning of Buddhism and the Value of Art' and 'The Religion of Art'. In both of them I used the word art in the wider sense, as including not only painting, sculpture, and architecture, but also fiction, drama, and music. In the first I argued that every genuine work of art enlarged the circle of our consciousness and it was in this enlargement that the value of art, from the spiritual point of view, consisted. Similarly, in the second I argued that art and religion overlap, inasmuch as there is in religion an element which is aesthetic and in art an element which is religious. The writing of these two articles made it clear to me, once and for all, that my love of poetry was not incompatible with my commitment to the Dharma. Henceforth I read – and enjoyed – the classics of Western literature, as well as the Buddhist scriptures, despite the frowns of puritanical fellow Buddhists.

Chapter Eight

A BANNER OF VICTORY

I DO NOT REMEMBER when or where I first heard the name of Padma-sambhava, the great Indian scholar and yogi who, in the eighth century CE, was mainly responsible for the initial dissemination of Buddhism in Tibet, was the founder of the Nyingma tradition, and about whose extraordinary personality there soon gathered a mighty corpus of myth and legend. I do, however, remember when and where I first saw a representation of Padmasambhava. It was not a picture I saw but an image, and I saw it in Darjeeling, in the Tamang Buddhist Gompa, towards the end of my first year in the eastern Himalayas. The gompa was situated in the heart of the Darjeeling bazaar and was, in fact, not a monastery but a temple of the typically Nepalese pagoda type, and I was taken to see it by some local Tamang Buddhists with whom I had become acquainted. I had not seen a Nyingma temple before, and I did not know quite what to expect. As I have written elsewhere, in words I cannot now hope to better,

> As I entered the temple, all the greater was the shock, therefore, when I saw in front of me, three or four times larger than life, the mighty sedent figure of the semi-legendary founder and inspirer of the Nyingma tradition, a skull cup in his left hand, a staff topped with skulls in the crook of his left arm, and the celebrated 'wrathful smile' on his moustached face. All this I took in instantly, together with the 'lotus hat', the richly embroidered robes, and the much smaller flanking figures of his two consorts, one Tibetan and one Nepalese. Having taken it in, I felt that it had always been there,

and that in seeing the figure of Padmasambhava I had become conscious of a spiritual presence that had in fact been with me all the time.

In other words, that magical figure had activated, at a very deep level, a part of me that hitherto had lain dormant and unrecognized. Though I had not seen it before, it was strangely familiar. It was familiar as my own self, yet at the same time infinitely mysterious, infinitely wonderful, and infinitely inspiring. Familiar, mysterious, wonderful, and inspiring it was to remain. Indeed, the Precious Guru was to occupy a permanent place in my spiritual life.

During the next few years I visited the Tamang Buddhist Gompa more than once, and got to know many members of the Tamang Buddhist community, especially two brothers, one of them an inspector in the West Bengal police who came to see me whenever his duties took him to Kalimpong. Unfortunately, neither of the brothers could tell me anything about the life and teaching of Padmasambhava, nor could any of the other Tamangs I happened to meet, whether in Darjeeling itself, in Kalimpong, or in the Duars. At the same time, there was no doubting the fact that, despite their almost total ignorance of their ancestral faith, the Tamangs strongly identified themselves not just as Buddhists but as *Nyingma* Buddhists, and no doubting the strength of their devotion to the figure of Guru Rimpoche, the Precious Guru. As I was beginning to realize, the ordinary Nyingma Buddhist, like the ordinary followers of the other forms of Tibetan Buddhism, was not historically-minded. He did not look *back* to Shakyamuni and Padmasambhava. Rather did he look *up* to a supra-historical 'archetypal' realm in which he saw the figures of a transfigured Shakyamuni, Padmasambhava, Avalokiteshvara, and Amitabha, the Buddha of Infinite Light, together with other divinities. In the Tamang Buddhist Gompa in Darjeeling the mighty sedent figure of Padmasambhava, flanked by his two consorts, occupied the central chamber on the ground floor, the 1000-armed Avalokiteshvara a smaller one on the first floor, and Amitabha a still smaller one on the second floor. Between them they represented the specifically Nyingma version of the Mahayana doctrine of the three bodies (*kaya*) of the Buddha, Padmasambhava being the emanated body (*nirmanakaya*), Avalokiteshvara the glorious body (*samboghakaya*), and Amitabha the body of Truth (*dharmakaya*).

In the little one-room Tamang gompa situated half way between Teesta Bridge and Kalimpong, the three figures were arranged in a row, on a low dais, Padmasambhava being in the middle, with a four-armed Avalokiteshvara on his right and Amitabha on his left. All three figures were of clay, life-sized, and painted in colours that had long since faded. On the one occasion when I set foot in the gompa I had the impression that in the eyes of the Tamang villagers who had built it, probably with their own hands, the three figures it enshrined were little more than the 'gods' of the Tamang community, to whom they made offerings and to whom they addressed their prayers. Even so, although the middle figure was of clumsy workmanship, as were the two others, it was instantly recognizable as that of Padmasambhava. There was the same lotus hat, the same wrathful smile, the same staff topped with skulls in the crook of the left arm, as in the very much larger figure in the Tamang Buddhist Gompa in Darjeeling, as well as in the figures, both large and small, in all the other Tamang gompas in the area. The Precious Guru's presence was in fact strongly felt throughout the entire Himalayan region. Not only were there gompas with his image wherever there were Tamangs or any of the other hill people who adhere to the Nyingma tradition. There were remote mountain caves in which the Precious Guru had meditated, and in which his image had been installed, so that the pilgrim, on looking in, would feel himself to be in the very presence of the Master. Places there also were, where the Precious Guru had performed miracles, or with which he was associated in other ways. According to Yogi Chen, the Chinese hermit who lived on the edge of the lower bazaar, with whom I was later to become acquainted, it was in Kalimpong that there had taken place the famous meeting between Padmasambhava and the King of Tibet, when Padmasambhava had demonstrated his superiority and the king had given his queen to be the Guru's consort. He had seen it all in his meditation, Yogi Chen told me. He also told me that beside the road, on the way to Tirpai, there was a large boulder. A demon had thrown it at the Guru, but the latter had headed it 'like a football', as Yogi Chen put it, and sent it flying.

Whatever the truth of these stories, Kalimpong was undoubtedly a special place, with a special atmosphere. Indeed, soon after my arrival there I was told that repeating a mantra once in Kalimpong was equivalent to repeating it a hundred times elsewhere. I was also told that in the atmosphere of Kalimpong an individual's true qualities, whether good or bad, developed more freely than anywhere else, and could more clearly be seen. Such being the case, one would have thought that among the Tamang Buddhists of Kalimpong there would be at least a few who were true inheritors of the Nyingma tradition, but so far as I could tell there were none. Though they definitely regarded themselves as Nyingmapas, and though they maintained some of the outward forms of their religion, they knew as little about the life and teaching of Padmasambhava as their co-religionists in Darjeeling and elsewhere.

The principal reason for this ignorance, it appeared, was that on their migrating from southern Tibet into Nepal, and acquiring the lingua franca of that country, the Tamang people had gradually lost their command of the Tibetan language and, in consequence, their ability to read the Tibetan scriptures and other religious works, including the very extensive literature of the Nyingma school. It therefore followed that if there was to be a renaissance of the Nyingma form of Buddhism among the Tamangs, there would also have to be a revival of Tibetan learning. What was no less important, they would need to have personal contact with the eminent lamas who had lately arrived in India as refugees from Chinese-occupied Tibet, especially with those who were versed in the Nyingma tradition. Jamyang Khyentse Rimpoche had, I knew, given teachings to local Buddhists while he was in Darjeeling, and no doubt his example was being followed by other lamas.

I do not know whether the Rimpoche ever visited the Tamang Buddhist Gompa during that time, or saw the mighty sedent figure of Padmasambhava that had affected me so deeply seven years earlier. But regardless of whether or not he saw it, at the time of his giving me the abhishekas of Manjughosha, Avalokiteshvara, Vajrapani, and Tara, the figure of the Precious Guru must have been present to his illumined consciousness, for not long afterwards he directed Kachu Rimpoche to bestow on me the Padmasambhava abhisheka. I do not remember when Kachu Rimpoche told me he had been so directed, but in any case it was not until 1962, three years after Khyentse Rimpoche's death, that I received the initiation. In the meantime I kept up my friendship with Kachu Rimpoche, or perhaps I should say he kept up his friendship with me, for he was more often with me at the Vihara than I with him at Pemayangtse Gompa. In fact, I visited him there only once. This was in November 1958. I was in Gangtok at the time, and at the invitation of Apa Pant, the Political Officer, had delivered five discourses on the *Hridaya-* and *Vajracchedika-Prajnaparamita Sutras*. These discourses were attended by the Maharaja of Sikkim, the Maharajkumar, Apa Pant, the Dewan of Sikkim, and officials of the Governments of India and Sikkim, besides a number of leading citizens of Gangtok. Among those who attended was tall, ruddy-complexioned Rai Bahadur Densapa, Chief Secretary to the Government of Sikkim, a staunch traditionalist with whom I was on very friendly terms. When I told him I wanted to visit Pemayangtse Gompa, he at once offered to provide the transport.

A day or two later I was riding up into the mountains of western Sikkim on a pony. This was only the second time in my life that I had ridden a pony, and despite the magnificence of the scenery by which I was surrounded, I did not enjoy the journey from the spot where I had left Densapa's jeep, the track being no longer motorable, to the ridge on which stood Pemayangtse Gompa, which I reached some hours later. This was not the fault of the pony, who seemed to know the way and carried me on and up at an even pace. The fact was that Theravadin cotton robes were not adapted to equestrian pursuits. Strictly speaking, the Theravadin monk should not even ride in a vehicle drawn by a horse, let alone ride one. Nonetheless, I had tied my inner robe like a *dhoti*, so as to be able to sit astride more easily. But this did not really help, as the saddle was simply a piece of sacking. By the time I arrived at my destination I was extremely sore, and moreover had the return journey later that day to look forward to.

Pemayangtse Gompa, 'Monastery of the Glorious Lotus', had been founded in the seventeenth century CE by Lhatsun Rimpoche, the learned Tibetan lama who was mainly responsible for the introduction of Buddhism into Sikkim, though according to legend Padmasambhava had been there before him and had, moreover, hidden, in different parts of the country, written teachings which certain gifted individuals would discover in future times when the world was in need of them. Lhatsun Rimpoche was a remarkable man. He was depicted in the religious art of Sikkim, I subsequently learned, as an ascetic. His blue-coloured body is almost bare. He is seated on a leopard-skin, his right hand makes the gesture (*mudra*) of teaching, his left holds a skull-cup, while in the crook of his left arm rests a staff like that of Padmasambhava. Besides introducing Buddhism into Sikkim, and founding Pemayangtse Gompa and other monasteries, Lhatsun Rimpoche started a line of tulkus or 'incarnate lamas' that continued down to the present, Kachu Rimpoche being the latest 'incarnation' and the eighth in the series. Though I was glad to see my friend, I was especially glad to see him at his abbatial seat. He was no less glad to see me, and received me warmly. In the course of my short visit I did not see the shrine-room of the monastery, so far as I remember, but in an upstairs room I did see a wonderful three-dimensional mandala in the form of a celestial palace. About six feet high, and made of wood, it was overarched by a painted wooden rainbow. As we were drinking tea in his room, Kachu Rimpoche pulled out from under his bed a large silver head of Padmasam-bhava. It was strikingly lifelike, for besides being a talented painter and sculptor the Rimpoche was a skilled metallurgist. Jamyang Khyentse Rimpoche had instructed him to make a life-size silver im-age of the Precious Guru, he explained. It was to be housed in a special roadside chapel, near the border with India, and its presence there would protect Sikkim from danger. We also discussed certain obstacles to the expansion of Buddhist work in the state, and in this connection Kachu Rimpoche informed me that a four-month refresher course for lamas was currently in progress at the monas-tery. The course was sponsored by the Sikkim Durbar, and seven-teen lamas were attending it.

One of the texts the lamas on the course may well have been study-ing was the traditional biography of Padmasambhava by his chief disciple, Yeshe Tsogyal. But be that as it may, in 1954 I received a review copy of a book which, to my surprise and delight, contained an epitome of the same traditional biography. The book was *The Tibetan Book of the Great Liberation*, the fourth volume in W. Y. Evans-Wentz's famous Oxford Tibetan series, and the epitome was the work of two Darjeeling-born Tibetans, the Sardar Bahadur S. W. Laden La and Lama Sonam Senge. Naturally I read the epitome before reading Evans-Wentz' long introduction to the volume, for I was eager to find out more about the facts of the Precious Guru's life than was already known to me from scholarly histories of Buddhism. With biographical fact in the ordinary sense, however, the epitome was little concerned. Its eighty-odd pages were replete with marvels and miracles, some of them quite bizarre, as when a dakini swallows Padmasambhava, having first transformed him into the syllable *hum*, and gives him the secret Avalokiteshvara initiation inside her stomach. In the review I wrote of the book as a whole I regretted that it had not been possible for the first comprehensive account in English of the great Guru's career to present him in a more balanced and, I believed, truer way as a thinker and saint rather than as a 'culture hero' and thaumaturgist. After all, numerous texts of great spiritual value were ascribed to Padmasambhava, one of them being included in *The Tibetan Book of the Great Liberation*, along with the epitome. The 'Great Liberation' of the volume's title in fact referred not to the colourful events of the epitome but to the goal of the meditative practices described in this text.

Though Laden La's epitome failed to enlighten me as to the historical biography of Padmasambhava, it nonetheless made me better acquainted with the 'symbolical' biography and more vividly aware of Padmasambhava the Myth, as distinct from Padmasambhava the Man. One might even say, as my friend Lama Govinda wrote to me, that so deeply did the great Guru impress the people around him that in their urge to convey his greatness to future generations they resorted to the superhuman and the miraculous. To Kachu Rimpoche the Precious Guru was not just a historical person, nor even a figure of myth and legend; he was a spiritual reality, and it was as a spiritual reality that he experienced him when he gave me the Padmasambhava abhisheka on 21 October 1962. By this time it was twelve years since my momentous first visit to the Tamang Buddhist Gompa in Darjeeling, and eight years since I read *The Tibetan Book of the Great Liberation*, and although the Precious Guru may not have been a spiritual reality to me, as he was to Kachu Rimpoche, I was at least beginning to have a sense of his spiritual presence.

The initiation took place in the shrine-room of the Vihara. Kachu Rimpoche came a few days earlier, bringing with him an attendant lama, as he usually did. His nephew Namzey, who was a little older than Dupchen, was already staying with me and attending the local high school. Both boys were on holiday just then, for it was the

Hindu festival season, and as the Rimpoche and I talked there could be heard coming from the bazaar the faint sound of fireworks. He had arrived early, partly in order to spend time with me, and partly because a day or two would be needed to make arrangements for the ceremony. These arrangements were in the hands of the attendant lama, who spent many hours making *tormas*, offerings sculpted from barley-flour dough, and decorated with discs of butter, each divinity having a torma of a particular size and shape. The butter-discs, I noticed, had to be moulded under water, since otherwise the warmth of the hands would cause the butter to melt. When finished, they were placed on a special table in front of the shrine, along with the other offerings and a variety of ritual objects. Among the ritual objects there was a beribboned arrow symbolizing Amitayus, the Buddha of Eternal Life (a form or aspect of Amitabha, the Buddha of Infinite Light), whose abhisheka Kachu Rimpoche would also be giving me. At length all was ready, and the Rimpoche and I took our seats on either side of the shrine, facing each other, the Rimpoche's seat being higher than mine and having in front of it a little desk for his dorje and bell and the other ritual items he would be needing in the course of the ceremony.

I cannot say that I remember much of the proceedings, which lasted two days. For most of the time I sat with closed eyes, simply allowing myself to become absorbed in the atmosphere of the occasion, an atmosphere to which the rather hoarse sound of the Rimpoche's voice as he chanted, the occasional tinkle of his bell, and the sharp scent of Tibetan incense, all contributed. I was very conscious of the fervour of the Rimpoche's devotion to Padmasambhava, and to the spiritual tradition of which the Precious Guru was the founder. I had once told Kachu Rimpoche that some Western scholars termed the Nyingma school the 'unreformed' school, as distinct from the other major schools of Tibetan Buddhism, all of which were 'reformed'. He replied that the Nyingma school was unreformed because it had never needed to be reformed, it having remained faithful to the teachings that had come from India during the first diffusion of Buddhism in Tibet. His devotion to the Precious Guru was very much in evidence when, towards the end of the second day, he explained to me how I was to visualize him in meditation. It was also at this time, I think, that he introduced me to the practice of the *mula* or 'foundation' yogas of the Vajrayana, and particularly to the Going for Refuge and prostration practice and the Vajrasattva visualization and purification practice.

It certainly was at this time that the Rimpoche – now my teacher as well as my friend – bestowed on me the name Urgyen (or Orgyen), the Tibetan variant of Uddiyana, the name of the country to the north-west of India where Padmasambhava was born – according to legend – from the calyx of a lotus flower. On this account he was known as Urgyen Padmasambhava, as well as being known by many other names. I was delighted to receive the name, which served to confirm my connection with the Precious Guru, as the abhisheka itself had done, besides suggesting that my true home was in the mysterious land of Uddiyana.

The morning after the ceremony I went to the bazaar, taking with me one of the Vihara's younger members. As I sometimes did, I had a look at a spot beyond the vegetable stalls where the Tibetans had a little street market. A man, probably a refugee, was squatting at the side of the road with a few items spread out in front of him on a piece of sacking. One of the items was a bundle of small Tibetan woodblock prints. As the man was asking only a few rupees for them, on an impulse I bought them, even though I could not read them and did not know what they contained. On my return to the Vihara I at once showed them to Kachu Rimpoche. They were all Nyingma texts, he told me, and the fact that I had come across them so soon after receiving the Padmasambhava initiation was a very auspicious sign. What was more, the longest of the texts was the well-known *Tharpe Delam* or 'Smooth Path to Emancipation', the author of which was a famous nineteenth-century Nyingma lama. It described the general and special preliminary practices of Atiyoga, to several of which Kachu Rimpoche had already introduced me. Before his departure the Rimpoche gave me further instruction regarding the Going for Refuge and prostration practice. I was to do it 20,000 times, though 100,000 times was desirable. He also gave me permission to make an English version of the *Tharpe Delam* with the help of Dhardo Rimpoche.

I knew that there was a certain amount of rivalry between the Nyingma school, to which Kachu Rimpoche belonged, and the Gelug school to which Dhardo Rimpoche belonged, but I nonetheless had no hesitation in asking the latter's help in making an English version of the *Tharpe Delam*, a Nyingma text. Apart from the fact that we were friends, and that I knew him to be free from sectarian exclusiveness, the tulkus of the line to which he belonged had been Nyingmapas until the time of his immediate predecessor, who had been educated as a Gelugpa on the orders of the Thirteenth Dalai Lama. He therefore readily agreed to help me with my task, and in the course of the next few months we spent many hours working together on the project, eventually producing a rough English version of the rather cryptic Tibetan text. Meanwhile, I made a start on the preliminaries to which Kachu Rimpoche had introduced me, beginning with the Going for Refuge and prostration practice. This was a quite strenuous practice, I found, and it was a couple of weeks before I could make a hundred prostrations straight off without becoming breathless and exhausted. But I persevered, and by the time I left for England I had accumulated the 20,000 prostrations that Kachu Rimpoche seemed to think was the minimum number required. Long before that, I had added to the Going for Refuge and prostration practice the Vajrasattva visualization and purification practice and the practice of offering to Padmasambhava a mandala or symbolic representation of the universe. I also continued to do the Green Tara sadhana I had received from Chattrul Rimpoche and the Manjughosha-stuti sadhana I had received from Jamyang Khyentse Rimpoche. All these practices required a good deal of time, as did the literary work in which I was engaged. I therefore decided that I had no alternative but to cut down my preaching tours in the plains. The result was that for the best part of two years I remained in Kalimpong, spending much of the day either at my desk or in the shrine-room.

My coming across the Nyingma woodblock prints so soon after receiving the Padmasambhava abhisheka may be regarded as an example of what Jung termed synchronicity, or 'the simultaneous occurrence of events which appear significantly related but have no discernible connection'. But as though one was not enough, there occurred around the time of my initiation another example of the phenomenon. One morning, a poorly clad Tibetan, evidently a refugee, came to the Vihara carrying a set of thangkas he wanted me to buy or, as he would have said, 'ransom', for things sacred were not to be bought and sold like so much merchandise. So far as I remember, he wanted a hundred rupees for the set. As gently as I could, I explained that I was not in a position to buy any thangkas just then, but the only result was that he lowered his price, thinking I was bargaining. This went on for some time, with me continuing to plead poverty and the wretched Tibetan again and again lowering his price. Eventually he reached a rock-bottom forty rupees. As it happened, forty rupees was all the ready money I had in the world at the time, but as the man was obviously desperate for money I bought the thangkas, feeling ashamed that I was getting them for so little and wishing I could have given more. There were eight thangkas in the set, and on unrolling them I found that they depicted the eight manifestations of the Precious Guru, one of them being none other than Shakya Seng-ge, the historical Buddha, who according to Nyingma tradition was the teacher of the sutras, whereas Padmasambhava had taught the tantras. Though I knew very little about thangkas, I could tell from the style that they were old, probably eighteenth century or earlier. They were mounted in tattered brown silk brocade, which in some places hung in strips. After inspecting them carefully, I hung them on the walls of my study-bedroom, five on one wall and three on the other, where they remained for the rest of my time in India.

In those days, refugees were arriving from Tibet all the time, some of them after experiencing terrible hardships on their way to the Indian border and safety. Officials and members of the aristocracy were often able to bring with them bullion and jewels (several bought houses in the town), but the common people and the monks had only the clothes they stood up in and, perhaps, their most valued possessions. These were generally of a religious nature, and included small portable shrines, thangkas, and images of Buddhas and Bodhisattvas. Some of the monks had with them quite large images that had belonged to their monastery and which they had managed to save from destruction by the Chinese troops. But whether lay people or monks, in Kalimpong there were no official arrangements to receive the refugees and no organized relief. Neither was there any work for them, though two enterprising monks who had been cooks at Drepung Gompa, the biggest monastery in

Tibet, opened a restaurant that quickly became the most popular in town.

Some of the refugees left Kalimpong for the plains, some begged, and some (a very few) turned to dacoity. But regardless of whether they stayed or went, most of them were forced, sooner or later, to sell even their most valued possessions for whatever they could get. It therefore was not long before the bazaar was flooded with images, thangkas, and other religious artefacts of every description. Most of them were bought by local Indian merchants for eventual sale in the West and in Japan. One such merchant took me to see his godown, which I found filled from floor to ceiling with rolled up thangkas. On another occasion a poorly clad Tibetan drew me into a dark front room and showed me a standing Tara, three feet high, with one of the most beautiful faces I had ever seen. He, or his master, wanted two thousand rupees for it, but for all the money I had, he might just as well have asked for two lakhs. The refugees, I found, like other Tibetans, often gave me first refusal when they wanted to sell something that had been consecrated, as they knew that being a Buddhist I would treat it with respect. For the first time in my life I found myself heartily wishing that I had more money and was able to ransom at least some of the many beautiful images and thangkas I was offered, for it grieved me to see them passing into the hands of non-Buddhists and being treated as though they were just another Tibetan export, along with wool, yak tails, and musk. At the same time, I was aware that even the most beautiful images and thangkas were simply aids to devotion and meditation, and that for me, as for every Buddhist, the most important thing in life was to get on with practising the Dharma and not waste time in idle regrets.

I was therefore glad when Kachu Rimpoche came to stay for a few days and see what progress I was making with the preliminary practices, thus reminding me what my true priorities were. It was in the course of this visit, I think, that I was reminded of the fact that my teacher was a visionary, and that he acted on his visions. One day he told me at breakfast that in his early morning meditation he had seen a banner of victory on the roof of the Vihara, and as soon as the meal was over he hurried off to the bazaar with his attendant lama. In the bazaar he went to a carpenter and had the six-foot cylindrical frame of the banner made; went to the cloth merchant and chose the red, green, blue, yellow, and white silks; found a tailor and had the silks made up into the flounces that would hang round the cylindrical frame; and finally returned in triumph with the banner and erected it himself on the roof of the Vihara with the appropriate ceremonial blessings. Hitherto, the only outward sign that our modest stone cottage was a Buddhist monastery was the Burmese gong that hung on the veranda and was struck at six in the morning and six in the evening every day, thus giving the time to the villagers who lived further down the hillside. But now we also had the five-coloured banner of victory, which proclaimed to all who saw it not any earthly conquest but the Buddha's victory over the forces of greed, hatred, and delusion.

Chapter Nine

THE SHADOW ACROSS SIKKIM

ON THE MANTELPIECE in the front room that was the Kazini's office there stood a framed head-and-shoulders photograph of an elderly gentleman of decidedly military appearance. There may even have been a row of medals across his chest. It was not long before the Kazini informed me that this imposing personage was Field Marshal Mannerheim, the father of modern Finland, and that he was her uncle. It was in fact he who had brought her up, and throughout her life she had been greatly influenced by him. Later still she confided to me that he was not her uncle, as she had been led to believe when young, but her father, and although she did not actually say so it appeared she was illegitimate. She always spoke of her supposed uncle, or real father, with great emotion, and seemed to have had a stronger feeling for him than for any other person in her life. She never spoke of her mother, but she often mentioned her sister (perhaps a half-sister) who lived in Edinburgh and with whom she was in regular correspondence. Her first husband she referred to only in passing, and always in connection with their life in Burma. I never learned his given name, for she invariably spoke of him simply as Langford-Rae, nor did I ever learn whether she was a divorcee or a widow when she met the Kazi. There was, however, a son of about my own age called Roderick, who worked in a tea garden in Assam, and who must have been born when the Kazini was in her early or middle twenties.

It was not easy to imagine the Kazini as a mother, either as a young woman or as the middle-aged woman she had become. There was very little that was motherly about her, though she was capable of showing genuine concern for those of whom she was fond. She once told me she had no maternal feelings and was quite indifferent to her son, whom she had probably handed over to the care of a Burmese ayah soon after he was born. Just how indifferent she was to him became evident when news came that Roderick had been killed in a road accident in Assam. His death had not affected her in the slightest, she assured me the next time we met, in a tone, and with an air, that suggested the event was of absolutely no interest to her.

She had displayed a similar lack of interest some months earlier, when Roderick came to see her in her new home. The Kazi received him kindly, and was his usual hospitable self, but the Kazini took no more notice of him than if he had been the most casual of casual visitors. So far as I remember, he stayed at the Himalayan Hotel, but though he came several times to Chakhung House, where I met him once, after the first visit it seemed he came to meet the Kazi rather than to see his mother. What was more, during his short stay in the town he somehow struck up a friendship with Joe Cann, whom he probably met in the lounge of the Himalayan Hotel, to which the scandalmongering old man was a frequent visitor. The Kazini had refused to have anything to do with him, for she knew, as I did, that during her 1950 visit to Kalimpong he had spread scurrilous stories about herself and Lha Tsering, and she thought it best to see as little as possible of one who possessed such an evil tongue.

Besides the photograph of the Field Marshal, there was also in the Kazini's office, and elsewhere in the house, another photograph in a silver frame. This was a studio portrait of a benign, gently smiling Kazi in traditional Sikkimese dress. It was the Kazini's favourite portrait of her husband, and it was she who had made him sit for it. She had made him sit for it not just out of wifely devotion but also in her capacity as his publicity officer, and over the years she must have distributed hundreds of copies of it among journalists, editors of newspapers, and other possible supporters. Unlike the Kazini, the Kazi never spoke about his father, nor did he ever mention his mother, but there were several occasions on which he talked to me about his two uncles, Phodang Lama and Khangsa Dewan, who I gathered had been powerful and influential figures in the Sikkim of their day and whom the Kazi evidently admired. He also talked to me about Chakhung, his estate in western Sikkim, with its orange gardens and its cardamom fields, and he once took me there for a couple of days. There were only servants living in the roomy old timber mansion, and when showing me round the Kazi directed my attention to the enormous brass *thalis*, more than two feet in diameter, that hung on the wall. Members of the family would eat from one of these giant plates, which would be carried into the room piled high with rice and meat. When they had eaten their fill it would be taken back to the kitchen, where the servants and other dependants would eat what was left.

Despite his feudal, aristocratic family background, the Kazi felt for the sufferings of the common people of Sikkim, regardless of whether they were of Tibetan, Lepcha, or Nepalese descent, and wanted to do what he could to improve their condition. This was one of the main reasons for his being in politics, the other reason being his hatred of the Maharajkumar, or Crown Prince, who now acted for his father, the Maharaja, and whom the Kazi was determined to 'finish off', as he once put it to me with uncharacteristic ferocity.

Before becoming friends with the Kazi and Kazini, I knew nothing about Sikkimese politics, even though I had been to Gangtok a number of times, but after becoming friends with them I came to know quite a lot. But perhaps I should say I *heard* quite a lot about the politics of Sikkim, especially from the Kazini, for I had no real interest in the subject and much of what I heard was soon forgotten. Nonetheless, there were things I heard so often I could not but remember them. Thus I knew that the political party to which the Kazi originally belonged had collapsed, that a new party had been formed, and that the Kazi was president of this party, that the party was opposed to the rule of the Maharajkumar, and that it was campaigning for the establishment of a democratic Sikkim. I also knew that the Kazi had the support of the Nepalese, who were the majority community in Sikkim, his two powerful uncles having encouraged Nepalese immigration into the country, that there existed a political party that supported the Maharajkumar, that the little Himalayan kingdom was a protectorate of India, and that the biggest player in the messy game of Sikkimese politics was the Government of India.

The Kazini was much more aware of the Indian dimension to Sikkimese politics than was the Kazi, even though it was he who went to Delhi for the purpose of explaining his party's position to officials in the Department of External Affairs. Besides being widely travelled, during her years in the Indian capital she had moved in political and diplomatic circles, had met many people, and was remarkably well informed. Like quite a few British officials in the days of the Raj, she preferred Muslims to Hindus, and for a time had been married to a Muslim, Dr Khan. They were married according to Islamic law, she told me, but since he would not agree to have a civil ceremony as well, she had refused to consummate the marriage and had left him. She was also decidedly pro-Pakistan, which meant she was correspondingly anti-Hindustan, and she admired the Socialist Party and its leaders much more than she admired the Congress Party and its leaders. Mahatma Gandhi she disliked, and in this connection she had a story to tell.

She had once attended one of the Mahatma's prayer meetings in the grounds of Birla House, where he was subsequently assassinated, and had found herself sitting directly behind him. As he listened to the scripture readings, she had studied him closely, eventually saying to herself, 'No, I don't like you.' Thereupon the old man had turned round and said, with a smile, 'You don't like me, do you, Madame.' She had been utterly astonished, and had not known what to say. It was as though he had read, or felt, her thoughts as she studied him. The Kazini told the story very well, wrinkling up her nose and shaking her head as she described how she had felt towards the Mahatma, for she was an excellent raconteuse, and could be very entertaining. She was also an excellent mimic, and I well remember her hilarious imitation of Pandit Nehru, the Prime Minister, absent-mindedly picking his nose as he presided over a public function. All things considered, it was not surprising that at their first meeting the Kazi should have been quite dazzled by the mature charms of the lively, articulate woman of the world, the like of whom he had not encountered before, though he was not so dazzled that he could not see she could be of great help to him in his political career.

In the event she proved to be a greater help to him that he could possibly have imagined. Besides being his public relations officer, she drafted his petitions and proclamations, did all his typing, and very soon was advising him and his colleagues on policy and tactics (one of the Kazi's favourite English words) and giving them the benefit of her legal knowledge and her intellectual acumen. In short, she threw herself wholeheartedly into what she had at first termed, rather disparagingly 'Kazi's politics', and identified herself with them to such an extent that she became, over the years, as great a force within the party as the Kazi, and at times a greater one. She was especially popular with the younger party activists, who were often at the house, for they liked the intemperate manner in which she denounced the Maharajkumar as a dictator and a tyrant and called upon them to overthrow his corrupt and oppressive regime. Like the Kazi, she spoke the language of democracy and human rights, but it was not a language that was natural to her; unlike the Kazi, she had no real feeling for the sufferings of the common people of Sikkim. She was very much the *grande dame*, and had she dazzled the Maharajkumar with her mature charms and married him instead of the Kazi (an unlikely event in view of the disparity between their ages) she would no doubt have thrown herself into *his* politics no less wholeheartedly than she had thrown herself into the Kazi's, and probably with greater satisfaction. Yet, here she was in Chakhung House, Kalimpong, and not in the Palace, Gangtok, and denouncing not Kazi Lhendup Dorje as a dangerous revolutionary but the Maharajkumar as a power-crazed dictator. She denounced him as a dictator so often and, to my mind, so unfairly, that one day I asked her how many political prisoners there were in Sikkim. This took the wind out her sails, for she was obliged to admit that there were no political prisoners in Sikkim. On another occasion the Kazi and I accused her of being a far bigger dictator than the Maharajkumar. We spoke laughingly, but she could see there was truth in the accusation all the same, and joined in the laughter, even though it was at her expense.

Although she worked tirelessly for the Kazi, and was such a force within his party, the Kazini did not appear openly on the stage of Sikkimese politics. She worked behind the scenes, preferring to help shape the script rather than to play any of the parts, even an important one. Letters over her signature did, however, appear frequently in the correspondence columns of the English-language Calcutta dailies. The letters were written in a lively, entertaining style, and often ridiculed the Maharajkumar's plans for the benefit of his country, and even the unfortunate ruler himself. The Maharajkumar felt this ridicule keenly, and whenever I was in Gangtok and staying at the Palace guesthouse he would complain to me bitterly about the Kazini's letters as soon as we met. He knew I could do nothing about them, nor did he expect me to, but was simply giving vent to his feelings. I did, however, once manage to convince the Kazini that a certain letter was libellous and should not be published. The Maharajkumar also once complained to me about the behaviour of Apa Pant, the Political Officer, a Chitpavan brahmin from Poona and a staunch Hindu. Pant had actually had the audacity to install, in the grounds of the Residency, a giant image of Hanuman, the Hindu monkey god. I already knew this, Pant having taken me to see the image the last time I stayed with him. The image faced north, he had explained, in the direction of Tibet, and the god's club was grounded, not shouldered, as a sign that India's intentions towards China were peaceful. But the Maharajkumar was not concerned with how Hanuman bore his weapon. What concerned him, and excited his indignation, was the fact that at a certain hour of the day the giant image's shadow fell across the Palace. 'Some people will think it's just foolish superstition,' he told me, 'but Pant believes in these things and he knows that *we* believe.'

I could not say that I believed in them, but I knew that India's shadow had fallen across Sikkim, and that in the eyes of the Maharajkumar the shadow across the Palace symbolized that bigger and darker shadow. Independent India was in expansionist mood, despite Hanuman's grounded club, and I very much feared that sooner or later, by one means or another, Sikkim would be absorbed into the Indian Union and lose its separate identity. I also feared that the Kazi and Kazini were unwittingly helping to facilitate this process with their activities. For his part, the Maharajkumar was bent on preserving Sikkim as a Buddhist kingdom with its own cultural and religious tradition and its own political structures, and in this he had my full sympathy.

Just as the Maharajkumar would complain to me about the Kazini's letters to the press, had any appeared since our last meeting, so whenever I returned from Gangtok she would want to know if I had met the Maharajkumar and, if I had met him, what had passed between us. She was not interested in our discussions about Buddhist activities in Sikkim, or the revival of the country's traditional arts and crafts. All she wanted to know was whether the Maharajkumar had talked about her and, in particular, whether he had complained about her letters to the press, for if he complained it would mean that their purpose – which was to hurt him – had been fulfilled.

The Sikkimese prince and the European lady indeed seemed to be obsessed with each other, even though they had never really met, as the Kazini was *persona non grata* at the Palace, and as the Maharajkumar, though he sometimes came to see me at the Vihara, never called at Chakhung House. Even the Kazi sometimes felt that the Kazini's preoccupation with the Maharajkumar's misdeeds, real or imagined, was excessive. Hers was indeed a character of the obsessional type, and during the time I was in regular contact with her it was with politics, in the sense of party politics and political intrigue and gossip, that she was obsessed, and apparently always had been. Outside politics she had, in fact, few interests. She was hardly ever seen in the bazaar, had no real social life, and seldom relaxed. If she did relax, it was either over a *thumba*, or bamboo beaker, of home-brewed millet beer, or over a book from her personal library. This little collection, which she had brought with her from Delhi, consisted mainly of political biographies and diplomatic memoirs. Her favourite author was Daniel Varé, a retired Italian diplomat, whose biography of the Dowager Empress of China she particularly praised.

The Kazini's obsession with politics, especially Sikkimese party politics, did her little good. Though she retained her robust appearance and her upright, almost regal bearing, it was an obsession that not only made her restless and anxious but soured her temper and frayed her nerves. Each time I returned from one of my preaching tours, which generally lasted four or five months, I could not help noticing that despite the powder and paint, her features were more drawn and haggard that when I had last seen her. She was always glad, even relieved, to see me, and although we had corresponded regularly during my tour she lost no time in telling me what had been happening in my absence, with special reference to the Maharajkumar's misdeeds and the Kazi's reluctance to follow her advice. There had already been differences between her and the Kazi with regard to what he and his party should do next, whether in the way of responding to events or precipitating them, and in course of time these differences became more pronounced and led to some angry exchanges. If the Kazini was a sledgehammer, the Kazi was a rock on which she often found it difficult to make an impression, which meant she was often an extremely frustrated woman. The frustration showed itself in a constant nervous drumming with her fingers on the table, or on the arm of her chair, and in the fact that she was irritable and impatient with her husband in minor domestic matters. Occasionally the frustration reached such a pitch that there would be an explosion, a stream of violent reproaches and angry recriminations would be directed at the Kazi, and he would find it impossible to reason with the Kazini or to calm her down. When this happened he would send a servant down to the Vihara with a verbal message requesting me to come up as soon as it was convenient for me to do so. I could always tell something was amiss from the way the servant spoke, and would therefore drop whatever I was doing and go up straightaway.

On my arrival at Chakhung House, the Kazi would disappear into the kitchen to order tea for me, leaving me alone with the Kazini, whom I once found prostrate on the drawing-room carpet, as though she had been biting it in her rage. On this occasion, as on the others when I had been sent for, she at once launched into a litany of complaints against the Kazi, the chief of which were that he never heeded her advice, that he listened too much to other people, and that he was incapable of making up his mind about anything. As I usually did, I listened to her for a while without saying very much, allowing her anger to exhaust itself, then gradually led the conversation away from the subject of the Kazi and into more peaceful and productive channels. Within little more than an hour she was her normal self. There were no traces of tears to be wiped away, for unlike other women she did not cry when she was frustrated, which was probably a mistake on her part, for the Kazi was a soft-hearted man, and tears might have had a greater effect on him than the tenth repetition of her point of view. Be that as it may, now that she was herself again the Kazi reappeared, a smiling servant brought in thumbas for him and the Kazini and more tea for me, and the three of us spent a pleasant hour together. The Kazini probably reminisced about her glamorous life in Delhi, and may even have referred to the Maharajkumar without too much acrimony.

Had the episode taken place in the summer of 1962, we must have talked about the Maharajkumar's forthcoming marriage to Hope Cook, a young American socialite whom he had met in Darjeeling two years previously. I was not interested in the marriage itself, which was attracting international attention and would no doubt be a colourful affair, but only in the fact that hundreds of pigs, chickens, and other living creatures were to be killed for the wedding feast. Since Sikkim was a Buddhist kingdom, with a Chogyal or Dharmaraja for its ruler, this seemed quite inappropriate, and I therefore wrote to the Maharajkumar protesting against the slaughter, as well as against the amount of alcohol that had been ordered. He replied at some length, maintaining that the number of animals to be killed, and the amount of alcohol that would be consumed, had been greatly exaggerated, and that age-old customs and traditions had to be kept up. This did not satisfy me, and the correspondence continued. While it was still in progress I happened to run into Princess Pema Tsedeun in the High Street.

'Why are you writing those dreadful letters to my brother?' she demanded, half-angrily and half-tearfully.

The Maharajkumar himself took my criticism in good part, and it was not long before I was having tea at the Palace with him and his new wife. What the Kazini wanted to know when I returned from Gangtok this time was not whether the Maharajkumar had talked about her and her letters, but whether I thought he and Hope Cook were in love, for it was widely believed that he had married her for political reasons. He was obviously very much in love with the lady, I told her, but whether she was in love with him I was quite unable to say.

Chapter Ten

TIBETAN TULKUS

I once asked Dhardo Rimpoche how many tulkus or 'incarnate lamas' there were in Tibet. He replied that there were about two thousand who were recognized as tulkus by the Tibetan government, plus an indefinite number who were regarded as such within their own district or their own monastery. Since the word 'tulku' was the Tibetan translation of the Sanskrit word 'nirmanakaya', and since 'nirmanakaya' meant the manifested or emanated body of a Buddha, I then asked the Rimpoche how many incarnate lamas were tulkus in this more exalted sense. After reflecting a moment he said, 'Perhaps six or seven.' The Dalai Lama and the Panchen Lama were the best known members of this much smaller group of tulkus, the Dalai Lama being the emanation of Avalokiteshvara, the Bodhisattva of Compassion, who was virtually indistinguishable from a Buddha, and the Panchen Lama of Amitabha, the Buddha of Infinite Light. All the rest of the two thousand, and perhaps some others, were tulkus in that they had been identified as the 'reincarnation' of a famous teacher or abbot who had recently died and who might, of course, have been far advanced on the path to Buddhahood. I later learned that a great teacher might decide to reincarnate in more than one body, Jamyang Khyentse Rimpoche, for example, being one of the five simultaneous reincarnations of the original Khyentse Rimpoche, the great nineteenth-century master.

During my fourteen years in Kalimpong, and especially during my time at the Triyana Vardhana Vihara, I had the good fortune to come in contact with many tulkus, and to receive initiation from some of the greatest of them. Even those from whom I received neither initiations nor teachings, but with whom I was simply on friendly terms, had a positive effect on me by virtue of their kindness and generosity. On the whole, tulkus were, I found, noticeably superior to the ordinary monks and lamas, some of whom were very rough characters indeed. Not only were tulkus more deeply versed in the Dharma: they were more cultured, and more refined in their behaviour. From the Tibetan point of view this was no more than was to be expected. After all, they were tulkus, with all that the word implied in the way of higher spiritual attainment.

I saw things a little differently. Though I did not doubt that at least some tulkus were what they were believed to be, I knew that tulkus were taken from their mothers at an early age, that they were brought up with the greatest care, and that they were surrounded by the constant loving attention of guardians and tutors who felt a deep respect for their young charges, and it seemed to me that all this must have played an important part in making them the exceptional human beings most of them were. Had they not been brought up in that kind of way, the spiritual qualities they had inherited from their previous lives might not have been able to find expression through the new psychophysical organism. I knew that the Sixth Dalai Lama had led a dissolute life. This was owing, it was generally believed, to the fact that for political reasons his birth had been kept secret for many years, with the result that he had not received the education that was customary for a tulku. Even the highest tulkus, it seemed, needed the right kind of education.

But regardless of whether or not it was the special education that had made them what they were, I counted myself fortunate in being in contact with so many incarnate lamas. What made it possible for me to be in contact with them was the fact that they were all in Kalimpong, where, thanks to Kashyap-ji, I happened to be living, and most of them were in Kalimpong as refugees. Like thousands of others, they had fled to India in order to escape from the Chinese army of occupation. The most important of these refugees was the Dalai Lama, whom I had the opportunity of seeing when his train stopped at Siliguri for an hour when he was on his way to exile in Mussoorie, in the Punjab hills. Three years earlier, when he and the Panchen Lama visited India in connection with the 2,500th Buddha Jayanti celebrations, I had not only seen him but met him several times – in Delhi, in Calcutta, and finally in Kalimpong, where I gave a reception for him at Everton Villa, where I was then living. Now he was again in India, this time as a refugee.

The story of his escape was a dramatic one. He had left Lhasa in the midst of the confusion created by the March 1959 uprising, when hundreds, perhaps thousands, of Tibetans were killed by the Chinese troops. He had left in disguise, under the cover of darkness, accompanied by his mother, his two tutors, and a few senior officials. For some days the world did not know where he was, or even if he was still alive. It was a time of intense anxiety on his behalf, especially among the Tibetans in Kalimpong and elsewhere, and I shared that anxiety. For many years I had not looked at the newspapers, but now I scanned them every day for news of the Dalai Lama. We eventually learned that after a difficult journey he and his little party had reached the safety of the Indian border, that they were in Assam, and finally that his train would be arriving in Siliguri the following day. The Kazi and Kazini and I drove down to the hot, dusty little township in the hope of our being able to see him, as did hundreds of Tibetans from Kalimpong, Darjeeling, and Sikkim.

It was a strange sight that met our eyes when we reached our destination. An enclosure had been built near the railway station, and within it stood the tall, maroon-clad figure of the Dalai Lama. Indian officials and their wives strolled in and out of the enclosure, talking among themselves, and taking no particular notice of the Dalai Lama, but no one else was allowed to enter. The Tibetans who had come to pay their respects to their leader were kept back by a barrier, which prevented them from coming anywhere near the enclosure. They could only gaze at him from a distance in mournful silence. For his part, the Dalai Lama could only gaze back at them. He had, I thought, a bewildered look, and I felt extremely sorry for him.

'He's not a refugee, he's a prisoner,' remarked the Kazini, rather loudly, probably in the hope that some of the Indian officials would hear her.

Not all the high lamas who were living as refugees in India, or in Sikkim, had escaped from Tibet in the same dramatic manner as the Dalai Lama. Some of them had left earlier, before the turmoil and bloodshed of the Lhasa uprising, and had made the journey without much difficulty. One of the most eminent of these was the Sixteenth

Gyalwa Karmapa, who according to his followers ranked third in the Tibetan Buddhist hierarchy, immediately below the Panchen Lama. His escape was a highly organized affair, and he arrived in Bhutan with a large entourage, and bringing with him many images, thangkas, and other precious items from his monastery in Tsurphu. For political reasons he was not allowed to settle in Bhutan, even though the Bhutanese were Kagyupas, as was the Karmapa, but he was allowed to settle in Sikkim, where he established himself at Rumtek. On his first – and so far as I know his only – visit to Kalimpong he stayed at the house of a wealthy Newar merchant, and it was there that the Kazi and Kazini and I met him. The Kazi had some business to transact with the Karmapa, and the Kazini and I were able to study him as the two men talked. He was of my own age, but decidedly corpulent, and he had, I thought, rather a shifty look. When the Kazini and I compared notes afterwards, we agreed that he seemed more like a successful businessman than a high lama.

This unfavourable impression did not prevent me from going to see the Karmapa when I happened to be in Gangtok at the same time that he was staying at the Palace Temple, where I had once met Jamyang Khyentse Rimpoche. He received me kindly, and at the end of the interview he presented me with a dorje and bell. They had been cast at Rumtek, he told me, and were from the first batch to be produced there under his direction. Unfortunately, despite his generosity, my impression of him remained unchanged. Tibetan Buddhists would no doubt have said that it was my own mental defilements that had prevented me from seeing the Karmapa as a Buddha, a fully enlightened being, and of course they might have been right.

There was no question of my seeing – or not seeing – Khamtul Rimpoche as a Buddha. Like the Karmapa he was a Kagyu incarnate lama, but unlike him he was a tulku of the middle rank, so to speak, and he lived unpretentiously with a close friend, who was also a Kagyu incarnate lama, in a little whitewashed monastery they had built at Rinkingpong, on a site from which one could see, in the far distance, the sunlit plains of West Bengal. Both were of my own age, perhaps a little younger, and both were by nature lively and friendly. I enjoyed their company, and I think they enjoyed mine. Once, when they were having lunch with me at the Vihara, a discussion arose about the Vinaya or code of monastic discipline. In the course of the discussion it transpired that my two friends were only shramaneras or novices, not fully ordained monks as I had supposed, and this astonished me. They, for their part, found my astonishment highly amusing, and could hardly contain their laughter. When I enquired the reason for their mirth, Khamtul Rimpoche spluttered, 'The Karmapa is only a shramanera,' and more laughter ensued. The Kagyupas, like the Nyingmapas, attached more importance to asceticism and the practice of meditation than to the observance of rules, though this was not to say that fully ordained monks were not to be found among them.

Rechung Rimpoche was the latest reincarnation of Milarepa's wayward disciple of that name, to whom the great poet-yogi addressed a number of songs, and at whose request he related the amazing story of his life. Thus he belonged to a line of Kagyu tulkus but, like Dhardo Rimpoche's predecessor, he had been educated as a Gelugpa despite his non-Gelug spiritual affiliations, though whether on the orders of the Dalai Lama I never learned. During the two years or more that he spent in Kalimpong, he stayed at Arunachal with my friend Peunkhang-sey, whose brother he was, which meant that he was often at the Vihara. Slightly built, with a pale face, and a worried look, he was of a scholarly bent and for a while had worked in London as a translator of Tibetan texts. So far as I remember, he returned to the West before my own departure from India. Though not himself a yogi, he was acquainted with the theory, at least, of weather-making, and once explained to me how rain was produced and how storms could be averted. He also gave me a dorje and bell. The handle, he said, was Tibetan, but the bell was Indian, having been cast at Nalanda centuries ago and brought to Tibet. The bell was smaller than the one presented to me by the Karmapa and had, I thought, a more silvery sound. On another occasion Rechung showed me a wad of thick black hair, about an inch in length. It was his teacher's hair, he told me, in a reverential tone. Unfortunately, I could not help exclaiming, 'It looks like a dog's hair!' Rechung said nothing, but I could see I had hurt his feelings and felt a pang of regret. But words once spoken cannot be recalled, and one has to live with the consequences – sometimes for the rest of one's life.

There was a third Peunkhang brother who, like Rechung, was a tulku and a Gelugpa, and who also lived at Arunachal. But that was the extent of the resemblance between them, and one would never have thought the two were brothers. Peunkhang Rimpoche (as I shall call him, having forgotten his name) was tall, heavily built, and slovenly, with a shock of stiff black hair that stood out from his head on all sides. As he came to me for English lessons, I soon discovered that he was not very bright. I also discovered that he was mentally disturbed. This was perhaps not unconnected with the fact that he believed he was not really an incarnate lama. 'No, I'm not a Rimpoche,' he more than once assured me, mournfully shaking his big head.

As I knew, the Peunkhang family belonged to the highest Lhasa aristocracy, and monks would sometimes identify a boy of such a family as the tulku of the late abbot as a means of ensuring the family's patronage for their monastery. This was probably what had happened in the case of my two friends, but whereas Rechung was able to act like a tulku, at least to an extent, his shock-headed brother seemed quite unable to do so.

Peunkhang Rimpoche was not the only tulku to have been wrongly identified, if that was indeed what had happened. In Darjeeling there was a refugee incarnate lama who had become a Christian and been given the baptismal name of David. I first heard about him from some of my Tibetan friends, who were scandalized that an incarnate lama, of all people, should have taken such a step, and they begged me to go to Darjeeling and convert him back to Buddhism. The next time I was in Darjeeling, therefore, I went to see David Rimpoche, as he was now known, and found him to be a healthy-looking young man whose principal interest was in body-building. Yes, he was a Christian, he acknowledged, but he didn't like the New Testament. He liked the Old Testament much better: it was full of fighting. The avowal did not surprise me, for I knew that the Tibetans in Kalimpong liked those films best which contained a lot of violence, such as the Westerns. David Rimpoche also disclaimed any wish to love Jesus. 'How can I love Jesus?' he demanded, 'I'm a man, not a woman.'

He evidently had a rather idiosyncratic understanding of Christianity, and I wondered what his understanding of Buddhism had been like. A few weeks later he was in Kalimpong, and I went to see him. This time he was not alone, but had an American woman sitting on his knee. I did not stay long, and we did not meet again.

With one exception, all the incarnate lamas I knew had been born in Tibet. The exception was Tomo Geshe Rimpoche, who had been born in Sikkim, and who was the tulku of a famous wonder-working lama who had died three or four years earlier. I first heard the name of this lama, the original Tomo Geshe Rimpoche, soon after my arrival in Kalimpong, when I visited the Tharpa Choling Gompa, the Gelug monastery at Tirpai, and saw in the main shrine-hall a photograph of his embalmed body. Two years later I heard much about him from Lama Govinda, who had been one of his disciples, and in 1961 I met the Rimpoche's 24-year-old reincarnation. He had been a prisoner in Lhasa for three years, and his arrival first in Gangtok, and then in Kalimpong, created a sensation in the area, for the name of Tomo Geshe Rimpoche was a name to conjure with not only throughout Tibet but throughout the entire Himalayan region.

We soon met, and soon became friends. He was probably the strangest and most mysterious person I have known. His form was that of a 12-year-old boy, but his behaviour was that of an old man, while the overall impression he created was one of innocence, wisdom, and gentle charm. More often than not a little smile of amusement played about the corners of his mouth. I sometimes visited him at his cottage near the Tharpa Choling Gompa, where he lived with his attendant monks and his little dogs. One day he showed me, in the narrow chapel behind his room, the meditation box in which his famous predecessor had spent so much of his time. The monks, I noticed, all went very much in awe of him, and though he spoke very quietly he was obeyed instantly, almost as though he had cracked a whip. Sometimes he visited me at the Vihara, especially after he had started studying English with me, when he came more regularly. Like all Tibetans and Sikkimese, he believed that whatever differences in rank and position there might be between them, the pupil always went to the teacher, not the teacher to the pupil. He already knew a little English, and made good progress. One day, quite spontaneously, he told me a little about himself and about his life as a prisoner of the Chinese.

He was born in 1937, he said, and at the age of seven had been sent to Sera, the Gelug monastic university near Lhasa, where he studied until 1959 and where he took his Geshe degree. He then moved to Lhasa, but hardly had he done so when the whole population rose against their Chinese oppressors, thus allowing the Dalai Lama to make his escape. As he happened to know many Amdopas, Khampas, and other Tibetans, the Chinese accused him of supplying them with life-giving *ribus* or 'magic pills', as well as of criticizing the Communist regime, encouraging opposition, and plotting with the Dalai Lama and other great lamas and with people in India. For this he was thrown into prison. What they said was true, he added, with a little smile. He *did* distribute ribus to many people. As I knew, both the old Geshe Rimpoche and the new were famous for their ribus, which were widely believed to have powerful protective qualities, and it is quite possible that the Chinese, despite their Communism, were still superstitious enough to have regarded them as a kind of alternative weapon and to have feared them – and their distributor – accordingly.

A prisoner of the Chinese for two years and three months, Geshe Rimpoche continued, he was being kept in different jails in Lhasa, and in one just outside Lhasa, a converted army barracks, where there were about 6,000 prisoners, some of them tulkus like himself. During his time as a prisoner he underwent two spells of solitary confinement, the first for fifteen or twenty days, the second for two months. His cell was about five feet square, and had neither a window nor a bed. Food was given to him through a hole in the door, which was kept locked, as was the door at the end of the passage. The guards told him he was being given the best food, such as no other prisoners were getting, for he was an Indian, and China was the friend of India. The food was rice and vegetables without salt. As the cell was of stone, he also suffered from the cold. After his first spell of solitary confinement he and about two hundred officials were kept together in three rooms. They were not allowed to talk about anything except the work they were doing for the Chinese, and they had to work all the time, with only a day or two off a month. He had worked for three months as a gardener, five months as a swineherd, four months as a washerman, and two months making envelopes, besides which he had stitched woollen belts, built and repaired walls, and worked in the fields.

The gardening work was fairly easy, though he and another man had to pull a heavy cart filled with earth. He also had to take out and put back a hundred heavy flower-pots, and he had to do this every day. (In Tibet, Geshe Rimpoche explained, flowers were always grown in pots.) He also had to water the flowers, and if any of them withered the Chinese would blame him. When he worked as a swineherd, he and another man had two hundred pigs to look after, especially when they produced young. The pigs lived in five sties, and the sties had to be cleaned out every day. He also had to cook both for the pigs and himself. As a washerman he had to wash the clothes of the military, both the men's and the women's. It was then winter, the water froze, and his hands became covered with sores. At first the clothes were washed in the river, but two prisoners who were working with him committed suicide by drowning, after which they had to wash the clothes in the streams. The clothes had to be perfectly clean, but if they used too much soap they were abused. When he was making envelopes he had to produce between 500 and 600 a day, and when he was stitching woollen belts he had to produce 120 a day. He stitched from six in the morning until ten at night. The work was difficult and affected his eyes.

At this point Tomo Geshe paused. It was difficult to relate all his experiences, he said quietly, a few moments later, and perhaps he had said enough. There was another pause, and I thought he must have finished, but at length he resumed his account of life as a prisoner in Chinese-occupied Tibet.

The Chinese made them work sixteen hours a day. They were given food only twice a day, morning and evening, together with a little water. One hour in all was allowed for eating. When he cooked for other prisoners, all he could give them was dried peas boiled in water. They not only had to work very hard; they had to work quickly. The implements with which they worked in the fields were of very poor quality, and soon broke; but when the implements broke they were accused of misusing the People's property and their rations were halved. Religious practice of any kind was absolutely prohibited. They were not allowed to eat while working, and the Chinese were always on the watch. Bad meat, which was not fit for consumption by the soldiers, was given to the prisoners. Though they could not sleep for hunger, they still had to work. The food was never enough. Sometimes they ate wild garlic while working in the fields. By eating it they could get a good night's sleep.

Geshe Rimpoche told me all this in a quaint mixture of Hindi, Nepali, and English, and in a quiet, matter-of-fact manner. As I listened to him, it seemed incredible that one so small and weak-looking could have endured so much hardship. It was no less incredible that in telling me about his life as a prisoner he should have shown not the slightest sign of ill-will towards those who were responsible for his – and his country's – sufferings. On the contrary, he twice told me that the work he did for the Chinese had been 'first class' (he used the English expression). It was as though he felt a quiet satisfaction in being able to work well under those appalling conditions, regardless of the nature of the work, for it showed he could rise above these conditions.

His story – though not his country's – had ended happily. Having been born in Sikkim, which was a protectorate of India, he was an India-protected person, and the Government of India had eventually been able to secure his release. Among those who heard, some months later, of Geshe Rimpoche's arrival in Kalimpong, was Lama Govinda, in his ashram in distant Almora. On coming to know that I was in personal contact with the Rimpoche, he wrote asking for more detailed news of his teacher, whom he had last seen, as a boy of nine or ten, in Gyantse in 1947, when they happened to pass each other in the street. In particular, he wanted to know whether Tomo Geshe remembered him, his old disciple, and whether he had recognized him at Gyantse. I replied at length, and was able to assure my friend that I had put his questions to Tomo Geshe, and that he had replied, quietly but firmly, 'I know him.' I also included in my letter a full report of the account Geshe Rimpoche had given me of his life as a prisoner of the Chinese, a report I wrote up from notes I had taken at the time. Lama Govinda used some of this information in the concluding chapter of *The Way of the White Clouds*, on which he was then working, and which after its publication in 1966 soon became a classic.

Geshe Rimpoche continued to study English with me until my departure from India. Before I left, he gave me a waistcoat that had belonged to, and been worn by, his famous predecessor. This was not a waistcoat of the ordinary Western type but a heavy woollen garment, maroon in colour, of the kind normally worn by Tibetan monks, with projecting shoulder-pieces and long lapels, one of which crossed the other. As befitted so great a lama, there were insets of red and gold brocade back and front. I do not know why my friend gave me the waistcoat, which most Tibetans would have regarded as a holy relic. Perhaps he thought it would keep me warm in the English winter, or perhaps he wanted me to have a link with his 'previous body' as well as with himself.

Tomo Geshe Rimpoche was not the youngest incarnate lama I knew. The youngest was the 16-year-old Pabongkhapa Rimpoche, the tulku of the great Gelug scholar of that name, who had been the teacher of Trijang Rimpoche, the junior tutor of the Dalai Lama, and of many other eminent Gelug lamas of the day. A strict follower of the Gelug intellectual and spiritual tradition, he was reported to have thrown Nyingma books and images into the river, but when I questioned Dhardo Rimpoche about this he was positive that Pabongkhapa Rimpoche had done no such thing. Photographs showed him to have been enormously fat, and his reincarnation, although so young, seemed to be well on his way to achieving a comparable girth. But he had a pleasant, open face, and was very bright. I once asked him which picture of the world was correct, the modern scientific one, or the traditional Buddhist one, with its Mount Meru, its four islands, and so on. Both pictures were useful, he replied, but they were useful for different purposes. I would have liked to see more of him, but he and his little party were on their way to one of the big refugee camps in South India, and they did not stay long in Kalimpong. Unfortunately, within six months of his arrival at the camp this promising young tulku died. The news of his death saddened me, and I wondered how long it would be before he was reborn.

Although I was in contact with many incarnate lamas, they were not always in contact with one another. In the case of some of them, this was because they belonged to different schools of Tibetan Buddhism, and had no previous experience of such contact. In the case of others, even those of the same school, it was bound up with questions of protocol, the strict observance of which was a feature of all aspects of Tibetan life. Who, for instance, was to make the first advance? Who was to call on whom, and with what degree of ceremony? I was exempt from all this. To the Tibetans of Kalimpong I was simply Imji Gelong, the English Monk, and contact with me was no more problematic for my tulku friends than contact with them was for me. Originally, some Tibetans had wanted to know whether I was a Mahayanist or a Hinayanist, for to all appearances I was a follower of the lesser path of individual emancipation. But once I had made it clear that despite my yellow robes I accepted the Bodhisattva ideal, and was a follower of the greater path of universal emancipation, I was warmly welcomed as a co-religionist.

One day it struck me that there ought to be more cooperation among the incarnate lamas I knew, especially the younger ones. They ought to work together for the good of Buddhism, and in this way encourage others in the area to do likewise. After consulting with Dhardo Rimpoche, I therefore invited twelve of them to the Vihara for a meeting. They all accepted the invitation, and on the appointed day all turned up as promised. Since at the Vihara they were on neutral ground, so to speak, there was no protocol to be observed, and they mingled happily with one another without regard to precedence. Some of them had not met before. I addressed them briefly, explaining why I had called the meeting, outlining my ideas about their working together, and appealed to them to give serious thought to the matter. My words were well received, and it was agreed that we should meet again in a few weeks' time for a fuller and more detailed discussion. That discussion was doomed not to take place. News of the meeting having reached the ears of the Tibetan officials in Dharamsala, to which the Dalai Lama had moved from Mussoorie, the Drunye Chenmo, or Lord Chamberlain, arrived in Kalimpong, called the tulkus together, and severely reprimanded them for presuming to hold a meeting without the permission of His Holiness. The tulkus were aware that the Dalai Lama probably knew nothing of the meeting at the Vihara, but the Drunye Chenmo spoke in his name, and there was no question of their arguing with him, or trying to explain their position. They could only hear and obey.

Dhardo Rimpoche, at least, was not surprised by the setback. He had his own experience of Tibetan officials, some of whom had tried to squeeze the Indo-Tibetan Buddhist Cultural Institute school out of existence and have the Rimpoche himself deported to Tibet on the grounds that, his father having been Chinese, he was a Chinese national. He had managed to avoid deportation by taking Indian citizenship. Later he went to Dharamsala, and in a private audience gave the Dalai Lama a full account of how the officials had harassed and persecuted him, speaking with a directness not at all in accordance with protocol. On hearing what the officials had done, the Dalai Lama's eyes had reddened with anger, Dhardo Rimpoche told me, and he had thrown up his hands in despair, exclaiming, 'But what can I do? What can I do?' On another occasion, when I had expressed a degree of astonishment that a certain incarnate lama should have in his entourage a man of rather dubious character, the Rimpoche added to my astonishment by declaring, 'The greater the lama, the worse the people by whom he is surrounded.' In the old Tibet, the great lamas – especially the major incarnate lamas – were powerful and wealthy figures, and those who hankered after power and wealth, whether monks or laymen, would often attach themselves to such lamas with an eye to their own advantage.

Apart from two or three who had studied English with me for a while, I was not acquainted with any Tibetan officials, though I often saw them walking through the High Street. They were easily recognized, not from anything distinctive in their appearance but from the way ordinary Tibetans behaved towards them, especially those newly arrived from Tibet. On passing an official, they would doff their hats, bend themselves almost double, and hasten past the lordly one with every sign of deference and submission. The official, for his part, would appear not to notice them. I observed, however, that after five or six months in India, the Tibetans no longer showed their officials such extreme respect. This was symptomatic of wider changes within the Tibetan diaspora. The officials had originally maintained that the Government of India should deal with the refugees only through them. They wanted the diaspora to be, in effect, a state within a state – a state that would be ruled by them in the name of the Dalai Lama. But this was an attitude that could not survive long in Nehru's India. The Drunye Chenmo belonged to a dying breed.

Chapter Eleven

THE ANNIHILATOR OF HELL

I first saw Dudjom Rimpoche at Rinkingpong. He had decided to build a three-storeyed Nyingma temple there, not far from the little Kagyu gompa, and I had been invited to attend the ceremony that marked the beginning of work on the project. This involved the burying of the earthenware pot containing various consecrated items at the spot where the temple was to stand, and it was Dudjom Rimpoche himself who performed the ceremony. Hundreds of people must have been present on that occasion, but I remember only the comparatively small figure of the Rimpoche, in his dark blue bokku, standing hatless in the bright sunshine on the edge of the hole in which the pot had been buried. He stood absolutely still, and I had the distinct impression that it was not just his a bodily still-ness. His mind, also, was absolutely still, as though the various winds that usually agitate the surface of our consciousness had in his case ceased to blow and he was at peace, in the deepest sense of the phrase, with himself and with the world.

Though I well remember where I first saw Dudjom Rimpoche, I have no recollection of when this happened. Probably it was towards the end of 1958. Even before that, however, I had heard much about the Rimpoche, who lived in somewhat regal style in a large house in the Development Area and was not often seen in pub-lic. In fact, an atmosphere of mystery surrounded him, and his name was generally pronounced in tones of awe. Though he was not the official head of the Nyingma school, he was widely regarded as its greatest living master and had many disciples, including some who were themselves eminent gurus. One of his disciples was my friend

Sonam Topgay Kazi, who was also related to him in a more mundane way, having married the Rimpoche's stepdaughter. It was probably Sonam Topgay who told me that before the workmen started digging the ground for the foundations of the new temple, Dudjom Rimpoche had solemnly requested all the ants and worms to depart lest they be killed or injured. Believe it or not, my friend added, the workmen later reported that in the course of their digging they had failed to come across a single ant or worm, whereas they would normally have expected to come across hundreds.

Sonam Topgay also told me, as did other Nyingmapas I knew, that Dudjom Rimpoche's wangkurs or Tantric initiations were particularly powerful and that this was well known. What they meant by 'powerful' in this connection was not altogether clear to me, and I suspected that the Tibetan word, like the English one, had acquired connotations which were not wholly in accordance with the Dharma. The Sanskrit term for Tantric initiation was *abhisheka* or 'sprinkling', but the pioneer Tibetan translators of the Tantric text chose not to translate the term literally. Instead, they rendered it as wangkur, which meant 'giving power' or 'empowerment'. When I started taking an interest in the Vajrayana, soon after my arrival in Kalimpong, wangkur – *wang* for short – was one of the first terms I heard in this connection, and I naturally wanted to know what it really meant, especially as I heard it so often. All that my lama informants were able to tell me, however, was that 'wang' meant becoming like a king, an explanation which left me no wiser than before. Eventually I discovered that the term abhisheka derived from the ancient Indian coronation ceremony, in the course of which water was poured over the king from four jars, thus investing him with the power to exercise the royal authority. Similarly, the bestowal of a wang empowered the disciple to study and practise the Tantra and thus attain Buddhahood more quickly than would otherwise have been possible. Some Tibetans, it seemed, believed that Tantric initiation involved a literal transmission of power from the guru to the disciple, so that the latter was more 'powerful' after the ceremony than he had been before it took place. I certainly did not experience a literal transmission of power when I received initiation from Chattrul Rimpoche and Jamyang Khyentse Rimpoche, nor was I to experience it later when receiving initiation from Dudjom

Rimpoche and other eminent lamas. When I received the Vajra-sattva abhisheka from Dudjom Rimpoche there was, however, a point at which I definitely felt something pass from him to me, but it was not something that could be described in terms of power.

I received the abhisheka on Saturday, 18 April 1959, a most auspicious day, for being the tenth day of the Tibetan month it was sacred to Guru Rimpoche. I did not receive it alone but in company with four other Buddhists, two of whom were Chinese and two English. The two Chinese, who came from Hong Kong, were Wu Chien, a monk, and Liu Fu Ken, a businessman. I did not know either of them, and I gathered that having heard of the efficacy of Dudjom Rimpoche's wangs they had come all the way from Hong Kong in order to receive initiation from him. Quiet, unassuming John Driver was already well known to me, but I had only recently made the acquaintance of John Blofeld. The latter was a tall, rather heavily-built man in his mid-forties, with a broad, florid face and a hearty, bellowing laugh. A lover of the East, especially its women, he worked for the British Council in Bangkok, had married a Chinese girl, and had two children who were at school in Darjeeling. It was in order to see these children that he was in the area from time to time. Previously he had always stayed with Joe Cann, who dissuaded him from coming to see me on the grounds that I knew nothing about Buddhism and was not worth meeting anyway. When *A Survey of Buddhism* appeared John therefore had a big surprise, came to see me the next time he was in the area, explained why he had not come before, and thereafter stayed with me whenever he visited Kalimpong.

On the present occasion he stayed with me for three weeks, walking with me up to Madhav Nikunj, Dudjom Rimpoche's residence, on the morning of 18 April and on the two following mornings. He had long been interested in Zen (in its Chinese rather than its Japanese form), as well as in Taoism, but having increasingly felt the need for a more devotional form of religious practice he had become interested in Tibetan Buddhism, and in particular in the Vajrayana. Receiving initiation from Dudjom Rimpoche would, he hoped, be the means of introducing him to that more devotional form of practice. John Driver was taking the initiation because he wanted to experience the Nyingma tradition from within, as a practitioner, as well as understand it from the outside as a Western scholar. Liu Fu

Sangharakshita (left) and Yogi Chen

Above:
Dudjom Rimpoche (left)
with Dilgo Khyentse
Rimpoche

Right: Dhardo Rimpoche

Left: Yogi Chen

Above:
Kachu Rimpoche

Right:
Jagdish Kashyap

Bottom left: Jamyang
Khyentse Rimpoche

Above:
Chattrul Sangye Dorje

Above: Sangharakshita with
Khantipalo and other friends
on the veranda of the Triyana
Vardhana Vihara

Below: Sangharakshita
addressing a public
meeting in Kalimpong

Ken, the businessman, believed that the practice of the Vajrayana would bring him greater wealth and prosperity. What Wu Chien expected to gain from the wang I did not know, but as he was a monk it must have been a spiritual rather that a material benefit that he was after. For my part, I welcomed the opportunity of forming a spiritual connection with a lama of Dudjom Rimpoche's eminence, about whom I had heard so much and who had made such a strong impression on me that day at Rinkingpong. Thus it was five people with very different backgrounds, histories, and aspirations who gathered in Dudjom Rimpoche's shrine-room that Saturday morning in readiness to receive the Vajrasattva abhisheka. It was Liu Fu Ken who had requested the initiation, and the rest of us had been invited to receive it along with him.

The Rimpoche sat on a kind of throne, his dorje and bell and other ritual implements within easy reach, while we, his five disciples, sat on the floor in front of him in a semicircle. The abhisheka proper, which in fact consisted of four separate abhishekas, did not take very long to complete. Like other abhishekas, it authorized those who had received it to study and practise a certain Tantric sadhana. Having given us the abhisheka, Dudjom Rimpoche therefore spent the rest of that first day, and practically the whole of the next two days, giving us a detailed exposition of the text of the sadhana to which the abhisheka pertained. According to John Driver, who provided us with a running English translation of the Rimpoche's exposition, the Tibetan title of this text could be rendered as 'The Essence of Profound Meaning: Being the One-Mudra Sadhana of Him Who Annihilates Hell'. In this context, 'Hell' signified not only the hell realm proper but also the animal realm and the realm of the pretas or 'hungry ghosts', in both of which there is more pain than pleasure. Similarly, 'Him Who Annihilates Hell' stood for Vajrasattva, the Diamond – or Adamantine – Being. He 'annihilates' Hell for those who have broken their vows and Tantric commitments by purifying them of the deep-seated mental defilements that were responsible for the infringements – defilements which, had the offenders not been purified of them, would have resulted in their being reborn in the lower realms. An exclusively Tantric figure, Vajrasattva was a Buddha appearing in Bodhisattva form. He was the Sixth Buddha, transcendent over time and space, and whether as the central figure of one of the mula-yogas or as the central figure of the Hell-Annihilator sadhana, he was associated with purification in the deepest and most radical sense of the term.

As we soon discovered, 'The Essence of Profound Meaning' was a very rich text, and Dudjom Rimpoche's exposition was not only eloquent and imaginative but scholarly. In the course of those three days we were introduced to the marvellous world of Mahayoga Tantra, one of the three divisions of Anuttarayoga Tantra. In the preliminary part of the sadhana, having recited a version of the Sevenfold Puja, one entered that world by invoking, then identifying oneself with, Vajrasattva in his wrathful Heruka form, dark blue in colour and in union with his light blue consort. From the point of contact between them, there springs a host of Wrathful Ones who, spreading and filling the sky, drive off and destroy all hindrances. They then coalesce to form an enormous vajra-tent, beyond which are three mighty barriers, the first of raging fire, the second of swirling black wind, and the third of violently agitated ocean waves. These fill the void in all directions, safely isolating one for the practice of the main body of the sadhana. This began with the production of the two bodhicittas, the relative and the absolute, the meditation on the three samadhis, and the generation of the Mandala of the Container and the Contained. From this point onwards, the sadhana consisted of a series of complex and colourful visualizations, all evoked by means of mantras and accompanied, in most cases, by mudras or 'hand gestures' of various kinds. The culminating visualization was that in which streams of nectar from the Buddhas of the Ten Directions and the Four Times, all in union with their consorts, fall upon the practitioner, purifying him of his mental defilements. His body, speech, and mind are then transformed into the body, speech, and mind of All the Buddhas, and his five skandhas or psychophysical aggregates into the five Buddha-wisdoms. The Hell-Annihilator sadhana concluded with the practitioner reciting the hundred-syllable Vajrasattva mantra and dissolving Vajrasattva, that is to say himself, into the void.

At the end of the third day, having finished his exposition of the Essence of Profound Meaning, Dudjom Rimpoche bestowed on us the fourfold abhisheka of Ekajati, Rahu, and Vajrasadhu, the principal guardian deities of the Nyingma tradition, explained how offerings were to be made to them, and gave us a copy of offering-prayers of his own composition. His work, in a sense, was finished; but ours had just begun. John Driver made a literal translation of the Tibetan text of the Essence of Profound Meaning, which John Blofeld turned into proper English, keeping as close to the original translation as English syntax permitted. The latter some years afterwards drew on this material for a book on the Vajrayana to which he gave what I considered the unfortunate title of *The Way of Power*. Our Chinese wang-brothers, for their part, made a Chinese version of the Hell-Annihilator sadhana which was published in book form. I took no part in these literary activities, except that I typed John Driver's translations of the offering-prayers and other material relating to Ma, Za, and Dor, as the Nyingmapas generally called the guardian deities of their tradition. I also commissioned small paintings of the Hell-Annihilator and the three guardian deities from an old Tibetan artist, a refugee whom Dudjom Rimpoche had recommended to me.

The Driver-Blofeld version of the Essence of Profound Meaning comprised twenty typed foolscap pages plus notes. I was glad to have it, and I was grateful to my two friends for their willingness to share with me the fruits of their joint labours. But much as the reading of it inspired me, reminding me as it did of our guru's exposition of the sadhana, I soon realized it was too long for me, especially as I was already practising two other sadhanas. I therefore went to see Dudjom Rimpoche and laid my difficulties before him. He responded with sympathy and concern, and at once promised to compose a shorter, simpler version of the sadhana for my especial benefit. He was as good as his word, and it was not many weeks before he gave me, written with his own hand, a copy of the promised text. John Driver, who was still in Kalimpong, translated it for me, on second thoughts replacing 'Hell-Annihilator' with the more euphonious 'Confounder of Narak'.

In the course of the next few months, I visited Dudjom Rimpoche several times, each time putting questions to him about the 'Order of Preliminaries to the Confounder of Narak', as my new sadhana was called, and each time received from him prompt and clear replies. Sometimes it was John Driver who accompanied me and acted as translator, sometimes it was my Tibetan disciple Prajnaloka. More than once we arrived at Madhav Nikunj to find scores of people –

men, women, and children – camping in the grounds or respectfully circumambulating the house, rosaries in their hands and mantras and prayers on their lips. Most of them were Sherpas, some of whom had come a long way in order to see Dudjom Rimpoche and obtain his blessing, for the whole Sherpa community was deeply devoted to the Rimpoche and regarded themselves as his disciples. How this had come about I did not know. He had evidently made a strong impression on them, but whether on account of his character and personality, or his great reputation as a Vajrayana master, or his being the current representative of a line of gurus to which they traditionally owed allegiance, it was not easy to tell.

Dudjom Rimpoche had certainly made a strong impression on me, both at Rinkingpong and as he expounded to my four wang-brothers and me the visualizations and other practices of the Essence of Pro-found Meaning. At Rinkingpong it was his absolute stillness which had impressed me, but in the Madhav Nikunj shrine-room it was his liveliness and spontaneity. These qualities showed themselves in his graceful, harmonious gestures, in the joyful, amused expression that lit up his soft, almost feminine features, and in the modulations of his rather hoarse voice. At Rinkingpong he had worn the simple, dark blue bokku that was his usual outdoor costume, but at home he per-mitted himself more freedom. Once or twice, when the weather was hot, he slipped his arms out of his bokku and sat with empty sleeves knotted round his waist in the rather swashbuckling style favoured by some Tibetan men. On another occasion – it may have been when giving the Vajrasattva initiation – he sported a Stetson and a colour-ful Hawaiian shirt, into the breast pocket of which was stuffed a thick wad of currency notes. His long hair was usually plaited into a braid and wound round his head. Sometimes he wore it spread out on his shoulders, which accentuated the rather feminine cast of his features, and sometimes, again, he tied it in a topknot like a yogi.

If at Rinkingpong Dudjom Rimpoche had seemed to be at peace, in the deepest sense, with himself and with the world, at Madhav Nikunj it was as though he took delight in being alive. It was a delight that had nothing to do with craving or attachment but was a purely spiritual emotion that had its source in a profound insight into the ultimate truth of things. He could be compared, in fact, to a great ocean, the depths of which were absolutely calm, but on whose surface innumerable waves danced and sparkled in the sunlight.

As well as answering my questions about the Order of Preliminaries, Dudjom Rimpoche explained that the text of the sadhana was extracted from one of the sections of a Nyingma tantra of the Mayajala class. The literal meaning of the Sanskrit word *mayajala* was 'net of delusion' or 'magic net', but its actual meaning, in the context of the Vajrayana, was 'Assembly (or Multitude) of Nirmanakayas and Samboghakayas'. The abhishekas for the practice of the sadhana were included in the Mayajala abhisheka but not vice versa. They were therefore properly styled Confounder of Narak sadhanas, *not* Mayajala sadhanas. Those who wished to practise the Mayajala sadhanas had to obtain the abhishekas of the hundred or so wrathful and peaceful deities, all of whom were emanations of Vajrasattva, who was the central figure of the Mayajala mandala.

In order to make perfectly clear to me the place of the Order of Preliminaries within the Nyingma system, the Rimpoche skipped down from his throne and, sitting beside me, drew on a blank page in my notebook a kind of genealogical tree showing how the Order of Preliminaries was affiliated to the Essence of Profound Meaning, this to one of the eighteen 'Elephant' tantras, and these to the Mayajala Tantra, one of the 'Great' Tantras, which itself belonged to a subdivision of Mahayoga Tantra, one of the three divisions of Anuttarayoga Tantra. He also explained that there were two lineages of Bodhisattva ordination, one going back to Nagarjuna and Aryadeva, the other going back to Asanga and Vasubandhu. The first was called the 'Profound View' lineage, the second the 'Extensive Activity' lineage. He also took the trouble of showing me how to make the mudras that accompanied the various offering mantras, demonstrating them in a graceful, fluid manner I could not hope to emulate.

For a year or two after this, I saw nothing of Dudjom Rimpoche, probably because I was away on tour for much of the time. I did, however, have news of him from time to time, and was one day shocked to hear that he had been arrested by the West Bengal police and was being held in custody in Siliguri. News of the arrest spread like wildfire among the Buddhists of the area, many of whom were not only shocked but puzzled and alarmed. Convinced that he had done nothing wrong, and that the authorities must have made a mistake, they demanded his immediate release. The Sherpas, faithful as ever, circumambulated the jail in which their guru was being held. Such of them as were familiar with the legendary biography of Padmasambhava may well have been reminded of the episode in which, having been falsely accused to the king, he is arrested, beaten, and bound to a stake and the wood heaped up around him set on fire. He is delivered by a miracle, Buddhas and deities coming to his aid. No miracles delivered Dudjom Rimpoche, unless it was by virtue of the fervent prayers of his disciples. He was released after a month without charge. Why he had been arrested in the first place nobody knew, but there were many rumours in circulation. One rumour was to the effect that Dudjom Rimpoche's wife had quarrelled with the Maharani of Sikkim and that the latter had engineered the Rimpoche's arrest in order to get even with her. According to another rumour, the arrest was due to sectarian rivalry, it having been brought about by Kusho Bakula, the Ladakhi incarnate lama who was both a Gelug monk and a Deputy Minister in the Government of India. I found it difficult to credit either of these explanations, or indeed any of the others I heard. The reason for Dudjom Rimpoche's arrest and incarceration remained a mystery to me, as did so much that went on within the Tibetan diaspora in Kalimpong.

In 1961 I renewed my contact with Dudjom Rimpoche, if indeed it had ever really been interrupted. He already knew about my work among the followers of the late Dr Ambedkar in the plains, and visiting him one afternoon in May, shortly after returning from my latest preaching tour, I asked him what would be the most suitable form of meditation for newcomers to Buddhism. In asking this question I had in mind those followers of Dr Ambedkar who had recently converted to Buddhism from Hinduism, in which they were treated as untouchables, and who wanted to practise Buddhist meditation. The Rimpoche replied that according to the Tantras there were three types of practice, corresponding to the three types of practitioner: low, middling, and superior. He then proceeded to give a brief explanation of each of the three types of practice in turn. The first type consisted mainly in the development of compassion for all sentient beings, inasmuch as in the course of the beginningless round of births and deaths, all beings have at one time or another been our fathers and mothers. In the second type, the practitioner visualizes a deity (a Buddha or a Bodhisattva) in front of him, then visualizes light coming from the deity's heart and entering him through the crown of his head. He also practises the four brahma-viharas or 'Divine Abodes'. In the third, the practitioner identifies his body, speech, and mind with those of the deity and reflects that all forms are the deity's forms, all speech the deity's mantra, and all mental states the deity's mind. All three types of practice begin with mantra recitation and conclude with dedication of merits.

Like all my Tibetan teachers, Dudjom Rimpoche, though he adhered firmly to his own tradition, was able to respect, even to appreciate, other forms of Buddhism. Thus when I asked him to be one of the speakers at a public meeting I was organizing in connection with the death anniversary of Jetsun Tsongkhapa, the founder of the Gelug school, he readily consented. That year the anniversary fell on the 2 December. On that day the famous golden image of Tsongkhapa was taken in a colourful, mile-long procession from the Tharpa Choling Gompa, Tirpai, to the Town Hall, where the meeting took place. The chief speaker was Trijang Rimpoche, who was then visiting Kalimpong, and whom I met several times. Also present on the platform, along with Dudjom Rimpoche, were Mindoling Doong Rimpoche, the titular head of the Nyingma school, Khamtul Rimpoche, Dhardo Rimpoche, Tomo Geshe Rimpoche, Pabong-khapa Rimpoche, and the new abbot of Tharpa Choling Gompa, who was studying English with me. Most of these lamas addressed the gathering, as did Parashmani Pradhan, a well-known figure in the Nepali literary world, Prajnaloka, and myself. In the course of his speech, Trijang Rimpoche remarked that a celebration of that kind had not been possible even in Tibet. It was, in fact, the first time that Tsongkhapa's death anniversary had been celebrated in India, and the significance of the occasion was marked by a truly record attendance. So great was the crowd that a thousand people, unable to gain admittance, had to listen to the speeches through the loud-speaker system outside the building. On the following day the image, having been reverently kept in the Town Hall all night, was taken in procession back to the Tharpa Choling Gompa, where a small function was held. I subsequently received a letter of congratulation from the Dalai Lama, who had probably heard about the celebration from Trijang Rimpoche.

Chapter Twelve

ARRIVALS AND DEPARTURES

The Triyana Vardhana Vihara was not a very big monastery; indeed, it consisted of little more than a four-roomed stone hermitage to which guest accommodation, in the form of a six-roomed thatched cottage, had been added. Running the Vihara nonetheless involved a good deal of work, especially as it was the centre of my Buddhist activities not only in Kalimpong but throughout the surrounding area and beyond. I therefore needed a helper, or at least someone who would look after the domestic side of things, supervise the cook, and deal with visitors when I was away.

The first of these helpers was Khemasiri, a Thai monk who had been staying with me at Everton Villa and moved to the Vihara with me. He was one of a group of four or five Thai bhikkhus who were studying at Shantiniketan, the rural international university started by Rabindranath Tagore, the famous Bengali poet, novelist, and dramatist. They were at Shantiniketan ostensibly to improve their English, but most of their time was spent together, when they spoke only Thai, with the result that, whatever else they may have learned, there was little improvement in their English. Khemasiri was very dissatisfied with this state of affairs. More single-minded than the other monks, and more determined, he realized that if there was to be a real improvement in his English he would have to give up his studies at Shantiniketan and move to a place where there were no Thais and where he would be forced to speak English. He had therefore come to join me at Everton Villa in 1956, arriving in time to help me organize the celebrations with which the Buddhists of Kalimpong marked the 2,500th Buddha Jayanti.

Khemasiri was a man of about my own age. Hard-working, and conscientious to a fault, he had a worried look that would deepen into a frown when he was concentrating. During his time at Everton Villa I helped him with his English, which improved considerably, and he was happy to assist me in various ways. When I moved to the hillside property that became the Triyana Vardhana Vihara he moved with me, for he valued our association no less than I did and wanted it to continue. Unfortunately, we had not been many weeks in residence when Khemasiri was taken ill. Tuberculosis was diagnosed, and he was admitted to the TB Sanatorium in Kurseong, a small hill station situated between Siliguri and Darjeeling. He was not at all happy there, and in a long letter to me he complained bitterly about the noise and confusion of the place and about the amount of quarrelling than went on. He was adamant that he did *not* have tuberculosis, despite the continued bleeding, and in letter after letter he spoke of his wish to return to Kalimpong and help me in my work, possibly accompanying me on my preaching tours in the plains. But it was not to be. Khemasiri's condition deteriorated, and the Thai consul in Calcutta made arrangements for him to be flown back to Thailand. The next letter I received from him was dated from the 'Hospital for Monks' in Bangkok. His health had improved, he wrote, and he was thinking of returning to India. I did not hear from him again.

For some months I was without a helper; but one turned up in the end, in the person of Sugatapriya, a young Theravadin monk from Assam. Like Khemasiri, he wanted to improve his English. Unlike Khemasiri, however, he was not very hard-working, and spent much of his time either lying on his bed or gossiping in the kitchen with the cook. He was one of those who appeared to believe that if they lived with me, their knowledge of the English language would increase automatically, and that they would absorb its grammar and vocabulary by way of a kind of pedagogical osmosis. Nonetheless, he made himself useful in various small ways, such as making out the weekly shopping lists, and for this I was grateful. He left the Vihara after little more than a year, no doubt thinking he had absorbed enough English for the time being. For the next two years I had no permanent, live-in helper, and had to make do with such occasional assistance as was forthcoming from Prajnaloka and from visiting Thai bhikkhus.

The Thai bhikkhus came from Shantiniketan and were the same group to which poor Khemasiri had once belonged and which he had felt obliged to leave if there was to be a real improvement in his English. They came during their summer vacation, for Shanti-niketan, a hundred miles north of Calcutta, was at that time of year unbearably hot and humid, and they were glad to escape to the cool of the hills. Junior to me in years, though not necessarily in ordin-ation, they were, possibly with one exception, more like students in yellow robes than real monks. But they were sociable and friendly, helped me in whatever ways they could, and joined me in the shrine-room twice a day for puja and meditation. With one of them in particular I became good friends. This was Maha Prom, a big, jovial, moon-faced Thai who was a little older than the rest, and who, after returning to Thailand a few years later, disrobed and became an officer in the Thai police. He and his companions often spoke of Thailand, which they very much wanted me to visit. Unlike India, it was a Buddhist country; monks were highly respected there, and were provided by a generous laity with every comfort and conveni-ence. Good preachers were especially appreciated, popular ones be-ing showered not just with robes and shoulder bags but with fountain pens, watches, cameras, radios, televisions, and, in short, with whatever was not expressly prohibited by the Vinaya. If I was to go to Thailand and deliver a few sermons, so they assured me, I would be richly rewarded, instead of having to give them for noth-ing, as in poverty-stricken India.

Thailand was a veritable paradise for Buddhist monks, it seemed! But I had no wish to go there, despite the tempting prospects held out to me by Maha Prom and the others; and I had no doubt, in any case, that Buddhism in Thailand would get on quite well without me. At the same time, I was intrigued by what I had heard. Did Thai lay people *really* give the monks television sets? And in that case, what kind of programmes did they usually watch? The lay people indeed gave the monks television sets, I was told. Nothing was to good for the monks, since they had given up the world (at least for the time being). Every monastery had a television set, at least in

Bangkok, and the favourite programmes were those devoted to Thai kick boxing – a vicious and potentially lethal sport.

Besides Thai monks from Shantiniketan, during the summer months the Vihara put up, at different times, two Vietnamese monks from the Nalanda Pali Institute (as it was then called) and a Ladakhi monk from Sarnath. Though all three were followers of the Maha-yana, they wore, as more in keeping with the climate and culture of India, the yellow cotton robes of the Theravada. Both Thich Minh Chau and Thich Thien Chau, the two Vietnamese monks, were studying Pali with my own teacher, Jagdish Kashyap, who, shortly after leaving me in Kalimpong with the parting injunction that I was to stay there and work for the good of Buddhism, had returned to his native Bihar and there established, not far from the ruins of the great Nalanda monastic university, its modest modern successor, the Nalanda Pali Institute. Minh Chau, who was very much the senior of the two, stayed for only a few days, but Thien Chau stayed for a much longer period. In fact he came more than once, and was with me during my final months in Kalimpong. A gentle, kindly soul, who got on well with the other members of the Vihara community, he not only gave me a good deal of help but gave it in an unobtru-sive, sensitive manner which made it doubly acceptable. In short, I found in him the ideal helper, and I hope he found in me someone worth helping. Like Minh Chau, he would have liked me to visit Vietnam, both of them having assured me that I would be welcome to teach at Van Hanh Buddhist University in Saigon.

Vietnam was traditionally a Buddhist country, its Buddhism being a combination of Ch'an and Pure Land teaching and practice. Since 1954 it had been divided into communist North Vietnam, led by Ho Chi Minh, and pro-Western South Vietnam, led by Ngo Dinh Diem, neither of which could be described as a paradise for Buddhist monks of any persuasion. President Diem was a Roman Catholic, as was his younger brother who was in charge of Intelligence and the Secret Police. His elder brother was the Catholic Archbishop of Hué. It was therefore not surprising that under the despotic regime of this unholy trinity, as under French colonial rule, the Catholic minority should have been supported and encouraged, while the less organ-ized Buddhist majority was discriminated against, suppressed, and finally systematically persecuted. In 1963 things came to a head. On

6 May President Diem issued an order prohibiting the Buddhists of Hué from flying the Buddhist flag on the Buddha's birthday two days later, even though a few days earlier, on the occasion of a Catholic festival, the Vatican flag had been flown all over the city. On 8 May, their leaders having failed to get the order rescinded, the Buddhists of Hué protested against the ban by going in procession from Tu Dam Pagoda to the radio station. Government troops broke up the procession with tear gas, then fired on the crowd, killing twelve people and wounding more than fifty. The monks, nuns, and lay people of South Vietnam then presented the Government with five requests, namely, (1) that the Government rescind the order prohibiting the flying of the Buddhist flag, (2) that Buddhism benefit from the same special treatment granted to the Roman Catholic missions, (3) that the Government stop arresting and terrorizing Buddhists, (4) that the Buddhist clergy and laity be free to practise their faith and to spread it, and (5) that the Government pay equitable compensation for the people killed and punish those responsible in a fitting manner.

These requests formed part of a manifesto, the concluding sentence of which read, 'We are ready to sacrifice ourselves until these reasonable requests are granted.' Diem did not find the requests reasonable, and events soon showed him and the other members of the Catholic oligarchy that the Buddhists meant what they said. As I have written elsewhere,

> On 11 June a 67-year-old monk burnt himself to death in a crowded
> Saigon thoroughfare in protest against the Government's
> persecution of the Buddhists. The monk, Thich Quong Duc, struck a
> match after his saffron robes were drenched with petrol and sat
> motionless in the meditation posture while the flames enveloped
> him.

It was an image that was flashed round the globe. Like thousands – perhaps millions – of other people I was struck by the erect posture of the old monk and his apparent insensibility to the flames swirling around him. Examples of such self-immolation for the sake of the Dharma were not unknown in the annals of Chinese Buddhism, of which Vietnamese Buddhism was largely an extension, the scriptural basis for the practice being a passage in the *White Lotus Sutra* in which a monk makes himself into a living lamp in honour of the Buddha. These accounts could be dismissed as mere legends, or as not meant to be taken literally. But it was not possible so to dismiss Quong Duc's act of self-sacrifice. That act had not been performed in an age remote from our own, nor did it feature in the colourful pages of an ancient sacred book. It had taken place in the middle of the twentieth century, had been witnessed by hundreds of people, and had been captured on film by a Western photographer. It was not easy to imagine the depth of spiritual practice that had enabled the 67-year-old Quong Duc to perform such a calm, deliberate act of self-immolation for the sake of the Dharma. I knew that I was devoted to the Dharma, and that for ten years and more I had worked for the good of Buddhism as enjoined by Kashyap-ji. But I was nonetheless aware that I did not possess a tithe of Quong Duc's faith and devotion, and I doubted if I would ever have been capable of making the supreme sacrifice he had made.

Be that as it might – for one never really knew what one was capable of – South Vietnam's Roman Catholic oligarchy remained unmoved by Quong Duc's death. 'If any more monks want to barbecue themselves,' Mme Nhu, the president's sister-in-law, told reporters, 'I'll be happy to provide the petrol and a match.'

More monks did want to 'barbecue' themselves, and in the course of the next few months, as the Diem government declared martial law, desecrated and destroyed major pagodas throughout South Vietnam, imprisoned thousands of monks and nuns, and held demonstrating students in concentration camps, eight more monks and one nun followed Quong Duc's heroic example. These events, which were widely reported in the Indian press, stirred me deeply, and I could not but empathize with the anguish of Minh Chau and Thien Chau as they heard of the sufferings of their fellow countrymen. But worse was to come. On 1 August the Diem government was overthrown by a military *coup d'état* in which both the president and his younger brother were killed. The United States government and the CIA were behind the *coup*, for Washington had become convinced that by persecuting the Buddhists, Diem was undermining South Vietnam's – and the United States' – fight against Communism. By the time I returned to England in 1964, the United States had begun its military involvement in the Vietnam war – an involvement that was to turn the country into an inferno.

Before that, however, on 22 November 1963, John F. Kennedy, the president of the United States, had been assassinated in Dallas, Texas. Like countless other people, I can remember where I was when I heard the news. It was a fine winter's day, with brilliant sunshine, cloudless blue skies, and a perfect view of the snows of Mount Kanchenjunga. I was on my way to the bazaar, and on passing the entrance to the Himalayan Hotel I caught sight of Annie Perry, the hotel's elderly proprietress, standing in the front garden. 'Have you heard the news?' she called out to me, 'President Kennedy has been shot.'

Though I have no similar recollection of the circumstances in which I first saw the picture of Quong Duc meditating amid the flames, that image nonetheless remains vividly present to me, a permanent reminder of what devotion to the Dharma really means. This devotion can express itself in a number of different ways, most of them much less dramatic than the old Vietnamese monk's. Lama Lobsang, the Ladakhi monk from Sarnath, expressed his devotion to the Dharma by acting as the guardian and teacher of the Ladakhi Buddhist boys who were students at the Maha Bodhi High School at Sarnath. When he came to stay with me he did not come alone. With him came another monk and more than a dozen of his young charges. I made the guest cottage over to them, so that they formed a separate unit within the Vihara community, doing their own cooking, and with their own daily routine of classes and outings and sessions in the shrine-room. Lama Lobsang was a Gelugpa, and a disciple of Kusho Bakula. Short, active, and good-humoured, he was perhaps ten years younger than me. I admired the way he handled the boys, who, it seemed, were all destined for the monastic life. Though he was a bit of a disciplinarian, not hesitating to cuff or slap them if they misbehaved, I could see that he loved them dearly and was utterly devoted to their welfare. He and the other monk were not of any help to me during their stay. Indeed, they were not in a position to be of help. But I was glad of their company, which made the Vihara feel more like a monastery and less like my own private hermitage.

I was also glad of the company, for three weeks, of Sister Amita Nisatta, who so far as I remember was the only woman ever to stay at the Vihara. Born in Sweden some forty years earlier, she had worked as a nurse, and was now a Theravadin nun, with a shaven head and yellow robes. As I had been relieved to discover, she was in temperament and behaviour very different from the turbulent and exigent French Nun, being calm, dignified, and undemanding. Though she spent much of her time either studying the Pali scriptures in her room in the guest cottage, or meditating in the shrine-room, she was by no means unsociable, and in the course of her stay we had a number of serious discussions about the Dharma – or Dhamma, as she would have said – and about the practice of meditation. These discussions seem to have made a deep impression on her, for she kept in touch with me until her death in Stockholm many years later. For my part, I remember her homely red face, and her warm smile, with considerable affection.

Sister Amita Nisatta may have been the only woman to have stayed at the Vihara, but she was not the only Western woman to have seen the place or even the only Western Buddhist nun to have done so. There was Sister Vajira, formerly Miss Eileen Robinson, from England. I had been familiar with her name since my earliest days in India, for she had published from Sarnath English versions of the first and second parts of the *Sutta-nipata*, and these were among the first books I bought after my arrival in the subcontinent in 1944. She was not a very educated woman, however, or even particularly literate. Having been left some money by an old lady she had nursed through her last illness, she had moved to India before the War, built herself a cottage at Sarnath, and become a Theravadin nun, her preceptor being a Sinhalese monk with whom I subsequently became well acquainted. By the late 1950s she was living in Darjeeling, and it was there that I first met her. She wore the maroon woollen robes of a Tibetan Buddhist nun, though I never knew whether she had received a Tibetan ordination or was simply adapting to the climate of the hills. Her straight grey hair was cut short, just covering her ears, and from behind her spectacles she looked out on the mad doings of the world with an expression of amused tolerance. After that first meeting I went to see her whenever I was in Darjeeling, and we corresponded regularly. From time to time she would enclose a small cheque with her letter, for she was a kind, generous woman who did much good in Bhutia Busti, the village on the outskirts of Darjeeling where she had settled.

It must have been through me that Sister Vajira came to know Jivaka. In any case, the transsexual English doctor confided his secret to her, presumably under the same 'seal of the confessional' that he had confided it to me. She had not been able to keep the secret for long. On one of her visits to the Kazi and Kazini, with whom she occasionally stayed, she had communicated it to the Kazini. According to the latter, it had slipped out one evening when Sister Vajira had partaken of her second thumba. The Kazini was less surprised to learn that Jivaka was a transsexual than she was mortified to discover, the next time we met, that I had known about it all along, and she reproached me for not having shared the information with her, an omission she seemed to regard as a breach of friendship. That Sister Vajira had communicated Jivaka's secret to the Kazini did not mean that the two women were at all close. Sister Vajira's plebeian manners jarred on the Kazini's more aristocratic sensibilities, while the high-handed way in which 'dear Kazini' dealt with people made Sister Vajira feel uncomfortable.

I was not surprised to learn that the English nun had partaken of a thumba when staying at Chakhung House. More than once, on my going to see her, she had appeared to be not quite herself. I had thought nothing about it at the time, but later I came to know that she was in the habit of following St Paul's advice and taking a little wine for the good of her stomach, except that the wine was whisky. This certainly did not lower her in the estimation of the local Buddhists, who being Nyingmapas did not have the same abhorrence of alcohol as their Gelug – and Theravadin – co-religionists. Indeed, the elderly head lama of Bhutia Busti Gompa, which was a sort of branch monastery of Pemayangtse, invited her to move into the gompa and live with him there as his consort. She accepted the invitation, and for two years she had a recognized place in the religious life of the local Nyingmapa community. At the end of that time she left the gompa with as little fuss as she had entered it, and moved into the wooden hillside chalet she had built for herself nearby. It was there that I saw her for the last time. She was an unusual woman, even a remarkable one, and I wish someone had written her biography. Her life ended tragically. She died when her chalet was swept away by a landslide in which dozens of people were killed.

After the departure of Sugatapriya, my second full-time helper, the Thai bhikkhus from Shantiniketan, Thien Chau from Nalanda, Lama Lobsang and his boys from Sarnath, and Sister Amita Nisatta all contributed to the ongoing life of the Vihara community, as did a number of other short-term guests from different parts of India and from abroad. It was only with the arrival on the scene of Lobsang Norbu and Thubden that I had the regular, full-time help I needed – had it, in fact, twice over, in that I now had two such helpers instead of one. Both were Gelug *getsuls* or novices, though only Thubden, the younger of the two, kept his head shaved and wore the maroon monastic robes. Lobsang Norbu had long since abandoned his robes and adopted Western dress. This was perhaps not surprising. In Tibet he had been a *dubdor* or 'fighting monk', with long hair on one side of his head, a smoke-blackened face, and robes worn in a distinctive way. He was proud of having been a dubdor, however. The dubdors were the true monks, he once assured me, very earnestly. Their only possessions were the clothes they wore and a small thangka of their *yidam* or tutelary deity. When I asked him what weapons they had, he replied, with great simplicity, that they had stick and stones. They practised stone throwing every day and he himself had been quite good at it. If they happened to kill anyone they had to disrobe and could not be a getsul any more. The dubdors were strict observers of the monastic law. They never went with women, though some of them had boys. He had never been anyone's boy, though he had been asked many times. The new abbot of Tharpa Cheling Gompa, who knew him well, would bear him out in this. I was not surprised that he should have been 'asked many times', for at twenty-seven or twenty-eight he was still good-looking, with a broad smile that showed his magnificent white teeth, and as a young dubdor he must have been doubly so, despite his soot-blackened face.

Thubden was recommended to me by his uncle, real or adoptive, with whom he had been living in the bazaar. This uncle, a small-time trader, was an ally of Dhardo Rimpoche in his resistance to the officials and a leader of one of the Tibetan factions in Kalimpong. He came to the Vihara one afternoon, bringing Thubden, and begged me to take him on. I was not anxious to have another mouth to feed, but reflecting that he must have consulted Dhardo Rimpoche about his nephew, and be acting in accordance with the Rimpoche's advice, in the end I agreed to give Thubden a place at the Vihara. It was not long before I was glad I had done so. Thubden turned out to be a very willing worker. In fact he enjoyed work. He particularly enjoyed serving me, whether it was washing my robes, cleaning and tidying my room, or airing my books, which in the damp weather quickly became mildewed. He and Lobsang Norbu worked well together, though there was a certain amount of rivalry between them, and I sometimes thought that Thubden was a little jealous of his older and more experienced colleague.

Lobsang Norbu was also recommended to me. In his case the recommendation came from Rechung Rimpoche, whose *chunzu* or estate manager he had once been. Having been connected with the Rimpoche, and through him with the aristocratic Peunkhang family, he was well versed in Tibetan etiquette and in the niceties of ecclesiastical protocol, and was therefore of great help to me in my dealings with incarnate lamas whom I did not know very well and who had to be treated with a certain amount of ceremony. He knew how many cushions should go to make up a particular incarnate lama's throne, and on what occasions a *khata* or ceremonial white scarf ought to be offered. Though still young, he had travelled widely in Tibet and had worked for a variety of masters. A monk was the best kind of master, he had found; the work was light, and you would be well treated. An unmarried layman was the next best; the work might be heavier, but you would not be treated too badly. The worst kind of master was a married man, for his wife would scold you and beat you, never allow you to rest, and try to get as much work out of you as she possibly could.

Lobsang's duties at the Vihara were certainly light, and I believe I treated him well. By Tibetan standards I probably treated him very well. He generally accompanied me when I went to the bazaar, walking a step or two behind me. He was always pleased when I went to see Dhardo Rimpoche, as I frequently did, for besides having a great respect for the Rimpoche he was on friendly terms with Gelong Lobsang, the Rimpoche's attendant monk, and liked to hob-nob with him while the Rimpoche and I talked. One day we arrived at the Old Bhutan Palace to find, chained up on the veranda of the upper floor where the Rimpoche lived, a fierce-looking Tibetan mastiff that lunged at us as we passed, barking furiously. Lobsang Norbu's eyes gleamed. 'That very good dog,' he whispered to me in English, 'If you ask Rimpoche, he give you that dog.'

I did ask Rimpoche, and he did give me the mastiff. He was not sorry to part with it, for it refused to live peaceably with the Rimpoche's little Tibetan terriers, which it clearly would have liked to tear to pieces, and its furious barking frightened the pet mynah the Rimpoche had taught to say *'om mani peme hum'*. Strange to relate, Lobsang had no sooner threaded a rope through the mastiff's spiked collar than it seemed to know we were now its masters and made no attempt to attack us. On the way back to the Vihara, though, it gave us a lot of trouble, especially when we passed through the High Street. It wanted to stop and fight every dog we encountered, so that it had to be dragged along bodily at the end of Lobsang's rope. I did not keep it for long, as it had to be kept chained up and Lobsang and I were the only ones who could go anywhere near it. Fortunately, we were able to find it a master who needed a fierce Tibetan guard dog more than the Vihara did.

Both Lobsang Norbu and Thubden could turn their hand to cooking in an emergency, as when the cook happened to be unwell, but they were rarely called upon to do so. The Vihara's first cook was Padam, an active, talkative Nepalese in his thirties who had worked for me when I was living at Everton Villa. He was a good cook, but too fond of the thumba, and a few months after Khemasiri and I moved into the Vihara I dismissed him for drunkenness. I remember him chiefly on account of his father, who was a *jhakkhri* or sorcerer. The old man once came to the Vihara to see his son. He was very decently dressed in traditional Nepalese costume, with a long black coat and a black pillbox hat. Whether due to age or illness he walked stiffly, yet he was very erect, and gave an impression of sinister dignity. The expression of his gaunt face and glittering eyes was very strange, and the Scottish Presbyterian missionaries who lived on the other side of town would probably not have found it difficult to believe that the withered old man was in league with the Evil One, or even that he was the Evil One himself. He died while Padam was still working for me, leaving his son with the problem of what to do with the paraphernalia of his sorcery. In the end, greatly fearing, he tied everything up in a cloth and threw it into the River Teesta.

Belief in sorcery was widespread among the Nepalese; there were many practitioners of the art, and it took many forms. One day, Durgaprasad came and told me that large stones, each of them marked with a cross or the figure 4, had been falling on the roof of their house out of a clear sky. His mother was greatly alarmed, he said. She believed that the family was being attacked by means of black magic and she appealed to me for help. He did not believe in black magic himself, my young friend added, but he had seen the stones falling and they definitely came from the sky. Having told him to assure his mother that I would do what I could to help, I went to see Dhardo Rimpoche. Someone was trying to harm the family, he said, after listening carefully to my account. The cross and the figure 4 both meant death. I was to leave it to him; he would see what he could do.

When Durga came to see me a few days later it was with the news that the showers of stones had ceased. But when I asked Dhardo Rimpoche what he had done he only laughed merrily and said, 'I just did a little puja.' Tibetan white magic had proved stronger, it seemed, than Nepalese black magic.

Padam was succeeded in the kitchen by a series of three or four short-term cooks, one of whom was known as Kazi. He was extremely dark, and so short that he had to stand on a stool in order to do the cooking on the kitchen range. He also had an unusually deep base voice. What I did not know when I engaged him was that he wanted to be a sorcerer. It therefore was not long before I heard coming from the kitchen, in the evening, the sharp 'tap tap' of a little drum. Kazi was trying to work himself up into a state of trance in which he would levitate, so I was told; but he never succeeded in doing this, and left after a few months – presumably to apprentice himself to a sorcerer. It was only with the appearance of Kaila that the Vihara had a permanent cook, that is to say, one who stayed for the remainder of my time in Kalimpong. Kaila was a 20-year-old Lepcha with a light, yellowish complexion and a shock of black hair. Like his predecessors, he did not live at the Vihara but came in each day. He was quiet and efficient, and besides being a reasonably good cook he knew a lot about crops and cultivation, which added to his usefulness. The Kazini strongly suspected that he colluded with my old brahmin sharecropper and that between them they cheated me of my full share of the makkai harvest. She was probably right, but I had learned not to look too closely into such matters. Complete honesty was no more to be found in the hills than in the plains.

Chapter Thirteen

THE CHINESE HERMIT

Sitting in my room one summer afternoon, I heard footsteps coming down the steep track behind the Vihara, and went out onto the veranda to meet whoever it might be. A few minutes later I was greeting, and being greeted by, a strangely assorted pair. One was a short Thai of indeterminate age, the other a thin, angular young Westerner who overtopped his companion by at least a head and a half. Both wore Theravadin monastic robes and carried begging-bowls.

The Thai visitor was Phra Vivekananda, with whom I was already acquainted. Though a student at the Nalanda Pali Institute, he was very different from the other Thai monks studying in India. Unlike many of them, he had not been made a novice as a boy but had become a monk when of mature age, after a rather turbulent secular life in the course of which he had been a professional kick boxer. He was still very fit, and liked to demonstrate kicks and jumps to anyone who was interested. Friendly and unpretentious, and deeply devoted to the practice of meditation, he was in many ways an ideal monk. His young companion turned out to be English. As I soon learned, his name was Jivaka, he was twenty-seven years old, and a year earlier he had been ordained in London as a Theravadin novice by a senior Sinhalese monk who had taken part in my own bhikkhu ordination in 1950. He had already visited Sarnath, Bodh Gaya, and Nalanda (where he had met Vivekananda), and he and Vivekananda had just spent a month travelling in Assam with other monks and meeting the local Buddhists.

The two visitors stayed for only a few days. Jivaka would have liked to stay longer, but he had promised the abbot of the Thai temple at Bodh Gaya that he would spend the Rains Retreat there, and the rainy season was fast approaching. Eighteen months later, however, he came and stayed with me for a much longer period. By this time – November 1961 – he had accompanied me on one of my winter preaching tours in the plains, had spent nine months in Bangalore with Buddharakshita, the companion of my early wanderings as a freelance ascetic, and had there been ordained as a bhikkhu and given the name Khantipalo, 'One Who Keeps Patient'. During his three years in India, Khantipalo spent altogether a year or more with me, either on tour in the plains or at the Triyana Vardhana Vihara. His time at the Vihara was interrupted by a three-month pilgrimage in Nepal, from March to June 1962, in the course of which he not only walked from Kusinara to Palpa Tansen, as Buddharakshita and I had done in 1949, shortly after our ordination as samaneras, but had continued on to Pukhara. Many of the Buddhists he met remembered me and my companion, and on one occasion Khantipalo was mistaken for me.

As I quickly realized, Khantipalo had been well-named by Buddharakshita. He indeed was one who 'kept patient', though I suspected he did not always find this easy. I also found him to be sincerely devoted to the monastic life, industrious, and willing – even eager – to learn. His only real weakness, so far as I could tell, was that he was rather lacking in self-confidence. Whether on tour in the plains or living at the Vihara we got on well together. Years later, in *Noble Friendship: Travels of a Buddhist Monk*, Khantipalo was to give a circumstantial account of life at the Vihara during his stay, including a detailed description of my daily routine. He had evidently been pleased to find in me an experienced senior monk who could communicate with him in his own tongue. 'It would be hard to imagine,' he confesses, 'what my own development in Dharma would have been like without [Sangharakshita's] example or his clear communication of the principles of the Dharma in a language that we shared.' Khantipalo also generously acknowledges that my explanations of Mahayana practices had immensely widened his horizons, and that his Dharma life had been enriched by living with me and slowly absorbing my teachings.

The relationship was by no means so one-sided as these comments might suggest. I gained a lot from Khantipalo's presence at the

Vihara, and when we were on tour, at least, he was of real help to me. Though differing in character and temperament, our social and cultural backgrounds were similar. Both were converts to Buddhism, and both were practising the Dharma in a foreign land and within the context of the monastic life. Thus we had a good deal in common. What we had most in common in the circumstances, apart from the fact that we were both Buddhists, was that we had the same mother tongue, English. Khantipalo was glad to have found a teacher who could communicate the principles of the Dharma to him in his own tongue. I was no less glad to have found someone *to whom* I could communicate the Dharma in my own language. This was not to say that Khantipalo had never 'heard the Dharma' from the lips of English-speaking Sinhalese and Thai monks, nor was it to say that I had never imparted the Dharma to English-educated Indian audiences through the medium of my own language. What it meant was that – other factors being equal – the Dharma was best communicated when speaker and audience, teacher and disciple, had the same mother tongue and were well nurtured in that tongue. Where this was not the case, either because the teacher was imparting, or the disciple was hearing, the Dharma in a language not his own, the Dharma would be less well communicated than it might otherwise have been and, unless special care was taken, misunderstandings would be bound to occur.

I loved to communicate the Dharma. Communicating the Dharma was one of the greatest joys of my life, especially when the communication was through the medium of the spoken rather than the written word. But I found it frustrating when I was not able to give full expression to my understanding of the Dharma, such as it was, because English not being the mother tongue of my English-educated auditors there was a limit to the extent to which they could follow me and a limit, therefore, to the extent to which I could communicate the Dharma to them. With Khantipalo there was no such limit, which made his companionship all the more welcome.

In his account of our life at the Vihara, Khantipalo notes that our devotion to the Dharma was expressed mostly through speech (puja, Dharma talk) and mind (meditation, contemplation) but little through the body. For me, at least, this was to change (or perhaps had already changed), as I took up the Going for Refuge and

Prostration Practice under the direction of Kachu Rimpoche. Our devotion to the Dharma was also expressed through literary work. At the time, I must have been writing the group of articles that became *The Three Jewels*, as well as producing, as usual, editorials and book reviews for the Buddhist monthly journal I edited. Khantipalo was no less busy. During his first few months at the Vihara, before he left for his Nepal pilgrimage, he was giving a final shape to *Tolerance, A Study From Buddhist Sources*, his first published book, materials for which he had started assembling while staying in Bangalore with Buddharakshita. The subject was one in which I was particularly interested, and I was therefore happy to discuss it with Khantipalo and to make a few suggestions.

There was a reason for my interest. It had not taken me long to discover, after my arrival in India, that on the subject of toleration, Hindus, in particular, had some confused and misleading ideas – ideas to which they clung tenaciously and which they did not like to have challenged. According to them, tolerance meant accepting that religions were all equally true, or were one in essence, or were all paths to the same ultimate goal (the variations on the theme were many), from which it followed that intolerance meant refusing to accept this 'essential unity of all religions' as it had been termed by one of its leading modern proponents. Hindus often criticized me for refusing to agree that there was no difference between Buddhism and Hinduism, for I found it difficult to believe that *atman* and *anatman* – self and no-self – were really the same thing, or that theism and non-theism were different aspects of the same truth. Nor was that all. Intolerance also meant criticizing other religions, as I indeed sometimes did, the assumption apparently being that such criticism was sure to be followed, sooner or later, by violence towards the followers of those religions.

In an essay entitled 'The Nature of Buddhist Tolerance', written ten years before my discussions with Khantipalo, I had sought to show that this was not true of Buddhism. Since they did not believe that all religions were true, the preachers of the Dharma felt free to criticize the false views (*mithya drishti*) maintained by the religions and philosophies they encountered, as the Buddha himself had done. At times they criticized them vigorously, drawing on all the resources of logic. Yet although they believed in the truth of their religion as ardently as any Christian bigot or Muslim fanatic, they never sought to impose it by force. The reason for their restraint was that Buddhism sees violence as springing from hatred, and hatred from ignorance. This ignorance was not merely intellectual, but spiritual, and consisted in the erroneous conception of 'things' and 'persons' as mysteriously ensouling an unchanging principle of individuality by which they were irreducibly differentiated from all other 'things' and 'persons'. By living in accordance with the Dharma, and practising its successive stages of ethics (*shila*), meditation (*samadhi*), and wisdom (*prajna*), the disciple transforms ignorance (*avidya*) into Enlightenment (*bodhi*), and hatred (*dvesha*) into compassion (*karuna*), which by its very nature cannot issue in violence. In the words of that early essay of mine,

> Buddhism, since it annihilates the erroneous conception of unchanging separate selfhood, stifles as it were ignorance, lust, and hatred in the womb, and permanently precludes the possibility of violence being used even for the advancement of its own tenets. The Dharma of the All-Enlightened and All-Compassionate One spares us the contradiction of spreading the gospel of love by means of the sword, and the paradox of burning alive men, women, and children who entertain religious opinions different from our own, to show how tenderly we care for the salvation of their souls.

Tolerance, A Study from Buddhist Sources, was not the only product of Khantipalo's pen during his stay at the Vihara. Like myself, he wrote articles and book reviews, some of them at my suggestion. He also wrote at least one letter to the press. In this he drew attention to the fact that certain Christian missionaries in Kalimpong were attempting the forced conversion of Tibetan refugee children. The letter was also signed by Sister Amita Nisatta, though I have no recollection of her staying at the Vihara at the same time as Khantipalo. After giving a colourful account of Dhardo Rimpoche's school at the Old Bhutan Palace, with its atmosphere of Tibetan culture and its cheerful-looking pupils in Tibetan costume, the letter continued,

> Contrast this with another school we saw, where instead of education in the rich tradition of Tibet, advantage is taken, by the Plymouth Brethren missionaries in charge of the orphans taught there. The missionaries admitted, to an emissary of the Tibet

Society, London, that they were not interested in educating the children or in teaching them handicrafts; they wanted only to convert them to Christianity. So that they are able to convert others, the children are taught Tibetan, Nepali and English.

The fifteen children we saw looked miserable and were ill-clad in European cast-off clothing. The atmosphere of the school-cum-orphanage seemed cold and cheerless. The children are kept strictly segregated from other Tibetans. Part of their time is occupied with the menial work of re-making the garden, though we were told that they were 'taught gardening'.

Worst of all, many of the school and house walls displayed vile anti-Buddhist posters which were banned from public boardings in Kalimpong by the Deputy Commissioner, Darjeeling. They are calculated to ridicule Buddhism in these Buddhist children's eyes and flaunt the claims of this narrow Christian sect as the only way to Salvation.

I had seen two of these posters a few weeks earlier. They were prominently displayed on the side of a little wooden building that I passed on my way to see Dhardo Rimpoche – a building I knew to be connected with one of the various Protestant missions. As I could not remember seeing the posters before, I stopped to take a closer look. Both were large and printed in black and red. One of them depicted a deep gorge, through which there flowed a mighty torrent. Two bridges spanned the gorge – one spun by a spider, the other a solid timber structure. A Tibetan lama pointed to the first bridge, above which was written, in Tibetan and English, 'Bridge of Good Works', while a Christian preacher pointed to the second bridge, on which was written 'Bridge of Faith in Jesus Christ'. Similarly, on the torrent was written 'Sin', on the cliff on the near side of the gorge 'the World', and on the cliff on the far side of the gorge 'Salvation'.

The other poster depicted a more dramatic scene, and needed no such explanations. On the left was a huge cross, cut deep into the solid rock. A young Tibetan girl was running towards the cross, and had almost reached it. Close behind her, also running, came an evil-looking Tibetan monk. He carried a knife, which he was about to plunge into the girl's back before she could take refuge inside the cross.

Tibetans who saw the posters were deeply shocked by them, as were other Buddhists of the town. They were particularly shocked by the second poster, with its infamous suggestion that Tibetan Buddhist monks were prepared to murder people in order to prevent them from becoming Christians. But though they were shocked by the posters, the Tibetans were reluctant to protest publicly against the denigration of their religion. Many of them were refugees, and they did not want the authorities to think of them as troublemakers. It therefore fell to me to do something about the posters. What I did was to write to the Deputy Commissioner, Darjeeling, whom in any case I knew, complaining that the posters were hurtful to the feelings of the Buddhists and requesting his intervention. I also pointed out that such posters were not conducive to harmony between the different communities of the town. The result was that the Deputy Commissioner wrote to the Subdivisional Officer, Kalimpong, whom I also knew, directing him to take action in the matter. The next time I passed the little wooden building, on my way to see Dhardo Rimpoche, I saw that the posters were no longer there.

Commenting on *Tolerance* forty years after its final shaping at the Triyana Vardhana Vihara, Khantipalo remarks, in *Noble Friendship*, that 'it is distinctly set against the view that Theravada represents the one true Buddhism as propounded to me by Buddharakkhita, for one, while presenting a very liberal view of all Buddhist traditions, in line with Sangharakshita's thought.' That liberal view was to be reinforced, during the months he spent with me after his return from Nepal, by our joint association with someone who, while generously sharing his knowledge of the Dharma with all who found their way to him, also refused to regard himself as a teacher or to accept disciples.

I must have first heard mention of Mr Chen in the mid-fifties, four or five years after my arrival in Kalimpong. Not that I then knew his name; all I heard was that a strange Chinese Buddhist was living in one of the larger buildings in the High Street, that he kept very much to himself, and that he was, in fact, a kind of hermit. An atmosphere of mystery surrounded the unknown Chinese Buddhist, at least so far as I was concerned. Joe Cann, who had met him once, told me that he did not welcome visitors, and that I should on no account try to see him. Some months later I learned that he had left his room in the High Street and was living in a bungalow situated on the edge of the Lower Bazaar. By this time I knew his name, and that he spoke English, and I resolved to call on him, despite Joe's warning. The worst that could happen was that he would scold me for disturbing him, or even refuse to see me. In fact, he greeted me cordially when I appeared on his doorstep late one afternoon, and invited me in.

Yogi Chen, as he came to be known, bore no resemblance to the austere, emaciated yogi of Buddhist and Hindu tradition. He was short and stout, with a chubby face that frequently wore a broad smile, and though no longer young he gave an impression of health and vigour. Far from being half-naked, he was decently clad in the Chinese-style shirt and baggy Chinese trousers that were, as I later discovered, his usual costume, though there were times when he would don the black gown and black skull cap of the Confucian scholar, or appear in the splendour of a sky-blue anorak and bright red baseball cap. He indeed spoke English, but his accent was so strong, and his mispronunciations were so frequent, that at times I found it difficult to follow him. Similarly, he did not always find it easy to make out who I was talking about when I mentioned the name of some Chinese Buddhist worthy of former times. 'Oh, you mean *so-and-so*!', he would exclaim, when he had puzzled it out, pronouncing the name in question very forcibly, with the correct tone. Out of politeness I never laughed at his mispronunciations, but Yogi Chen had no such inhibitions and laughed heartily at mine, which he seemed to find highly amusing.

These little difficulties over pronunciation did not really obstruct the flow of communication, and that evening I learned quite a lot about Yogi Chen. I learned that he never left 'The Five Leguminous Tree Hermitage', as he called his tiny bungalow after the five such trees that once stood before it, in whose place there were now five bamboo poles with prayer flags; that he spent the whole day meditating, except for the half-hour he devoted to literary work; that he had published several books in Chinese, including a volume of poems; that he had studied with many Tibetan gurus; that he was vehemently opposed to Communism; that for him Red China was 'Slave China'; and that he did not encourage visitors. Before I left, however, he told me I was free to visit him from time to time, and that I should come in the late afternoon or early evening. During the

next four or five years, therefore, few months passed without my
paying Yogi Chen a visit, if I was in Kalimpong, and I learned to
appreciate the extent and variety of his meditative experience and
the clarity and precision of his understanding of Buddhist doctrine.
Occasionally, with his permission, I would take someone to see him,
and thus it was that late one afternoon in the summer of 1962 I made
my way to 'The Five Leguminous Tree Hermitage' not alone but
accompanied by Khantipalo.

The three of us probably discussed meditation, for it was either on
this occasion, or shortly afterwards, that Yogi Chen undertook to
give Khantipalo and me a talk on the subject. Whether this was his
own idea, or the result of a request by his two yellow-robed visitors, I
no longer recollect. Whichever it was, the talk proved to be a long
one. It was given in weekly instalments, over a period of more than
four months, and five years later it came out in book form as *Buddhist
Meditation, Systematic and Practical. A Talk by the Buddhist Yogi C.M.
Chen.* That the talk could be thus enabled to reach a much wider
audience was almost entirely due to Khantipalo. It was he who took
down Yogi Chen's words in longhand, sometimes scribbling furiously in order to keep up, and whom our host therefore designated
the Writer. My task was to listen carefully to the talk, with a view to
supplementing, and if necessary correcting, Khantipalo's written
record, and I was accordingly designated the Listener. Yogi Chen's
own designation, as the giver of the talk, was the Speaker. A photograph taken by Lobsang Norbu through the window of the room
where our sessions took place shows the three of us at work. Two
vertical window bars divide the photograph into three panels. The
middle panel of this triptych is occupied by Yogi Chen, who sits on a
small *moira* or wicker stool. His head is bowed, as though in thought,
and he holds a prayer-wheel. The right-hand panel is occupied by
me, in profile, and the left-hand one by Khantipalo, who is bent over
his notebook; we both sit on chairs. There is a certain dynamic in the
picture. I am turned fully towards Yogi Chen, who is turned slightly
towards Khantipalo, who, though he looks down, is half-turned towards Yogi Chen.

Khantipalo and I always arrived at the Five Leguminous Tree
Hermitage for our weekly session at about 5 o'clock. Sometimes we
came through the rain, for the rainy season had now set in. If we

happened to be a little late, we would catch a glimpse of Yogi Chen peering round the curtain of his shrine-room window, on the lookout for us. The sessions lasted for between two and three hours, depending on how long Yogi Chen spoke and how much discussion took place, after which the Writer and the Listener had a forty-minute walk back to the Vihara, either through more rain or, perhaps, under the stars. The next day, the subject still being fresh in mind, Khantipalo converted his notes into a rough draft which he gave to me for my comments. After being revised in accordance with my suggestions, the draft was typed and then taken along to our next meeting with Yogi Chen. He read it carefully, adding and deleting where necessary. In this way a faithful version of what he had said was finally arrived at.

Buddhist Meditation, Systematic and Practical contained seventeen chapters, each chapter corresponding to a talk, or – as Yogi Chen saw it – to an instalment of one and the same talk. The seventeen chapters covered the principal meditations of the Hinayana, the Mahayana, and the Vajrayana, which Yogi Chen, in common with the followers of all schools of Tibetan Buddhism, regarded as successive stages of the path to realization of the three 'bodies' of a Supreme Buddha. One of these chapters covered meditations of the Chinese Mahayana schools, another covered Ch'an ('Is Ch'an a meditation? No!'). Before he gave his first talk on meditation, however, Yogi Chen gave the Writer and the Listener an outline of his biography. It would be a good introduction to his explanations of practice and realization, he told us. Though it was only an outline, it took Yogi Chen a whole evening to deliver it, and when *Buddhist Meditation, Systematic and Practical* was published it made a useful introduction to the book. In accordance with Tibetan literary practice he divided his biography into four parts: (1) Outward Biography, (2) Inward Biography, (3) Secret Biography, and (4) Most Secret Biography.

The Outward Biography was the shortest of the four. That is, Yogi Chen spent less time talking about it than he did talking about any of the others. There were eight children in the family, four girls and four boys, of whom he was the youngest. Most of his siblings died young, and one day an itinerant fortune-teller told his mother that he, too, would have a short life. His parents frequently quarrelled, for his father not only took a second wife but was always running after the wives of others and squandered the family income on women and drink. For these reasons Yogi Chen grew up with two fears, the fear of death and the fear of poverty. One of his duties when young was to look after his grandfather, who had a shop, and the old man became very fond of him on account of his diligence. But he became nearly blind, and practically everything had to be done for him; he also developed consumption, and when Yogi Chen was ten he died. As a young prince, the Buddha-to-be saw the Four Sights – the old man, the sick man, the dead man, and the wandering ascetic – in the city outside his home – the Speaker told us with evident emotion – but *he* had seen three of them *inside* his home. The fourth, a bhikshu, he did not see at that time. He had no need of the Hinayana scriptures to convince him of the first Noble Truth, the truth that conditioned existence is suffering. Nonetheless, he could not give up the world, as there was no one else to look after his parents.

The Inward Biography was the story of his secular and religious education. It began when he studied with a teacher well-versed in the Confucian classics. As he had a good memory, he was always placed first in the class of ten boys. After finishing his study of the Five Classics, he joined the town's newly opened Government Primary School. While the school taught the usual range of subjects, he liked to study and recite poetry with a young man who had risen to official eminence through the old imperial examination system but had renounced it all in order to live as a hermit in the mountains, as he afterwards did. His poems were a mixture of Buddhism and Taoism, with a strong element of his own renunciation. After attending Primary School and High School, the young Chen went for six years to the Normal School in Changsha, the capital of Hunan Province. Since he wanted to learn everything, there was little he did not put his hand to, even playing the piano! His room had no light, so during the night he studied in the one place where a light was always burning – in the latrines. Though his health suffered, he was in this way able to graduate well and to obtain a post as a teacher in the High School. Later he was appointed Secretary to the Provincial Education Committee, a post for which altogether 142 candidates from all over the province had competed. The appointment gave him access to the Provincial Library, which was an extensive one, and he had the opportunity to read widely. He particularly liked the Taoist authors, with their promises that there were many different methods for prolonging life. One day he consulted a Taoist diviner, who predicted that if he followed their teachings not only would his life be prolonged but he would become immortal. This was a turning-point in his life, Yogi Chen solemnly assured us. From then on he was less concerned with worldly things.

The library contained the works of T'ai-hsü, the leading Chinese Buddhist monk of his day, and he read them with enthusiasm, for with their blend of the modern scientific attitude and ancient wisdom they were easy for an educated young man to read. At that time there was no lay Buddhist organization in the province, and at the urging of a group of upasakas he wrote to T'ai-hsü, inviting him to come and help them form one. A correspondence ensued, in the course of which T'ai-hsü gave him a Buddhist name and told him he should become his disciple. Two or three months later, the famous monk arrived in Changsha and a lay Buddhist association was formed and soon flourished. A temple for the worship of Amitabha was built, and T'ai-hsü himself founded a Buddhist college, in which his new disciple worked under his direction. It was around this time, Yogi Chen subsequently wrote to Khantipalo, that he began studying the *Avatamsaka* or 'Flower Ornament' Sutra, being particularly interested in the chapter on Pure Conduct, which explains how all the activities of daily life are to be accompanied by the bodhicitta. So captivated was he by this chapter that he wrote it out in a fine, vigorous style of calligraphy so that many copies could be printed for free distribution. Nonetheless, the Speaker sadly confessed that evening, he still continued to oscillate between Buddhism and Taoism, for he thought that, good as the Hinayana was, it could not prolong his life. Though he had taken the Buddhist Refuges, he really forsook them when he met a Taoist guru and learned some life- prolonging practices from him. The guru had the face of a little boy, though he was very old, and he had taken no food for twenty years. Though initially sceptical, after staying with the guru for a few days he could believe what he was told. He himself was then eating only vegetarian food and living apart from his wife (the Speaker had not mentioned her before).

During this period, he met a teacher belonging to the Gelug trad-ition, Gelu Rimpoche by name. Being a Gelugpa, he laid great emphasis on the observance of the Vinaya or code of monastic dis-cipline, as well as on the four foundation yogas of the Vajrayana. As taught by him, the four were Going for Refuge, Prostration, Reciting the Hundred-Syllable Mantra of Vajrasattva, and the Offering of the Mandala. Since he could not do these practices while living in the midst of his family, he went to live in a shrine in his teacher's temple. Each of the foundation yogas had to be performed 100,000 times. In the course of two or three years he was able to perform the first three foundation yogas 100,000 times each, but he had time to perform the fourth, the Offering of the Mandala, only 10,000 times in that place and he was still engaged in making up the total here in his hermitage in Kalimpong.

Gelu Rimpoche had heard that in the Guangxi region there was a great Nyingma guru who lived as a hermit, and he went to see him. On his return he would not reveal to him and the other disciples what he had learned, and Yogi Chen therefore decided that, although it would leave his family short of money, he would go and see the guru himself. While he was with him, Lola Hutuktu, as the guru was called, gave him many instructions regarding the practice of meditation, including Mahamudra and Dzogchen. Lola Rimpoche predicted that he would have a daughter, and told him to eat meat and live with his wife. He also told him to practise Ch'an, for its realization went very deep.

Yogi Chen's Inward Biography concluded with his telling us that he had had altogether four kinds of guru. They were the outward guru, the inward guru, the secret guru – who gave instruction in meditation and in dreams – and finally the guru of the Dharmakaya, which was the wisdom of non-guru. This guru was not a personality, but from it he had obtained many teachings. So saying, the Speaker rose from his seat and went to a glass-fronted cupboard packed with books. Taking out a good pile of them, he brought them to us to see. In all there were twenty-two volumes, the pages of each one of them covered with closely written Chinese characters. They were ex-amples of what the Tibetans called 'mind-treasures' and were on a variety of subjects, including the chakras and bodily health.

Coming to his Secret Biography, Yogi Chen began by emphasizing the importance of understanding that we must achieve perfect renunciation, and that our desire to practise must always be strong. When he was working as a teacher, for example, he used to spend the summer vacation and the Christmas holidays as a hermit. He did this for many years. When the time came for him to return to school he always wept, for at school there would be little time for meditation, but he knew he must earn money to support his aged parents and his own family. Many times he tried to leave home and live like Milarepa, the Tibetan solitary, and he often wanted to become a bhikshu, but each time worldly obligations held him back.

On one occasion the Heruka Dakini came to him when he was half awake and told him, 'Go to Szechuan.' He went there and received detailed teachings of the Vajrayana. At another time, while he was meditating, the Five Sisters, emanations of Buddha Amitayus, told him to go to Sikang. Fortunately, he was able to raise the money for the journey and set out for Sikang where, on the snowy mountain, he received instruction from the famous Ganga Guru. He stayed with him for a hundred days, constantly practising his teachings, and left only when his money ran out. While he was staying there, the Karmapa appeared to him in a dream and told him to come to him at Derge, in Tibet. Wei-to, his guardian deity, promised him 50,000 Chinese dollars to meet the expenses of the journey (the Speaker laughed heartily at the recollection), and in fact he was able to raise exactly that amount. Before he arrived at Derge he had a vision, one night, of Jamyang Khyentse Rimpoche, who was the teacher of the young Karmapa. In Derge he received many teachings from the Rimpoche, teachings that were not always imparted to the other disciples. From this time onward he gathered numerous abhishekas and instructions from seven different schools of Tantra in Tibet. The practices had their corresponding texts, which might be read and studied only by those who had been given the abhishekas for the meditations they described. Naturally, such texts were never published, their contents being meaningful only to those who had received instruction in them. It was also worth noting, Yogi Chen added, that not all his teachers were famous or enjoyed established reputations. The majority were little known, lived in remote, wild places, and had few disciples, if any. Those who were not tulkus might, by their efforts in this lifetime, establish a line of tulkus. Very often the deepest teachings were to be found among gurus of this type.

At the end of this period of seclusion, his gurus asked him to return to his home province to rescue his family from the turmoil of World War II. This he did, and after he had settled his family in a safe part of the country, he spent two years living in a cave. A wealthy supporter who wanted to go on pilgrimage to India suggested that they should go together. This they did in 1947, when they made the pilgrimage to the principal Buddhist holy places. His kind supporter then returned to China, but Yogi Chen stayed on in India, where he spent one week meditating in each of the holy places in order to find out what would be the best place for his practice. Finally, his supporter helped him to remain in India, so he came to Kalimpong and to the hermitage in which he was now living.

The subject of the Most Secret Biography was Realization. This had three divisions, Yogi Chen explained, corresponding to the three yanas of Tibetan Buddhism. The three were the Attainment of Cause, in which renunciation was most important; the Attainment of Path or Course, in which understanding of impermanence was necessary; and Attainment of Consequence, in which there was certainty of Enlightenment. Under these headings, Yogi Chen described how he had practised renunciation, how he had lived as a hermit for altogether eighteen years, and how the practice of meditation had brought glimpses of Truth.

Chapter One of *Buddhist Meditation, Systematic and Practical* was entitled 'Reasons for Western Interest in the Practice of Meditation'. It corresponded to Yogi Chen's first talk on meditation, the previous week's talk – on his biography – having been of an introductory nature. There were four reasons for this interest on the part of Westerners. (1) The Dharmakaya embraced the Dharmadhatu, and neither East nor West was outside it. All could receive its blessing and all, wherever they happened to be, could practise Buddhist meditation. (2) Many Buddhist sages had predicted that Buddhism would spread to the West, where a basis for it already existed in the form of the ethical teachings common to all religions. (3) Christianity was in decline in the West. (4) Western daily life was very stressful.

Chapter Two dealt with the real and ultimate purpose of meditation, while Chapter Three was concerned with the exact definition of terms relating to meditation, both its theory and its practice. The ground having been cleared, the fourteen remaining chapters covered between them the entire field of Buddhist meditation, from the five basic meditations, which are the antidotes to the five mental poisons, to the highest meditations of the Tantra. Each chapter began by paying homage to a particular Buddha or Bodhisattva, guardian deity, or guru, or to a particular group of such beings, just as Yogi Chen had done before he gave the talk on which the chapter was based. Chapter Nine, for example, which was on the Four Foundations of Mindfulness, began with a homage to Je Tsongkhapa, the Four Agamas, and the Five Hundred Arahants. Both the Writer and the Listener noticed that these acts of homage on the Speaker's part were no mere formality but gave expression to a very real sense of devotion. Besides recording Yogi Chen's words, Khantipalo introduced each chapter with a short paragraph or two in which he set the scene, as it were, for the evening's talk. He also interpolated short accounts of any discussions that had arisen in the course of the talk, as well as any comment by me.

Shortly after completing his work on *Buddhist Meditation, Systematic and Practical*, Khantipalo left for Thailand, there to pursue his study and practice of the Dharma under traditional Theravadin auspices. Before his departure, we were associated in two events which in their different ways were of special significance to us both. Quite early in his stay, I had introduced Khantipalo to Dhardo Rimpoche, whom he soon came to admire for his kindness and generosity, and for the way he looked after the 200 or so pupils of his school, many of whom were the children of refugees. When I told him that Dhardo Rimpoche had agreed to give me the Bodhisattva ordination, therefore, he was moved to ask the Rimpoche if he, too, could take the ordination.

I had been attracted to the Bodhisattva ideal for almost as long as I had been a Buddhist, and I had been a Buddhist for twenty years. During that period, texts like 'The Vows of the Bodhisattva Samantabhadra', which forms part of the *Avatamsaka Sutra*, and Shantideva's *Shiksha-samuccaya* or 'Compendium of Instruction [for Novice Bodhisattvas]' had thrilled and inspired me, and my feelings had found expression in poems and articles, as well as in Chapter Four of *A Survey of Buddhism.* There were two reasons for my being so strongly affected. As I have written elsewhere,

> In the first place, there was the sheer unrivalled sublimity of the Bodhisattva ideal – the ideal of dedicating oneself, for innumerable lifetimes, to the attainment of Supreme Enlightenment for the benefit of all living beings. In the second, there was the fact that, as enjoined by my teacher Kashyap-ji, I was 'working for the good of Buddhism', and that I could not do this without strong spiritual support, the more especially since I received very little real help or cooperation from those who were supposedly working with me. This spiritual support I found in the Bodhisattva ideal, which provided me with an example, on the grandest possible scale, of what I was myself trying to do within my own infinitely smaller sphere and on an infinitely lower level.

Thus it was not surprising that on 12 October 1962 I should have received the Bodhisattva ordination, especially as by that time I had been working for the good of Buddhism for twelve years, both in Kalimpong and the neighbouring hill towns and in the plains. It was also not surprising that I should have received the ordination from Dhardo Rimpoche, whom I had known since 1952 and whom I had come to revere as a living Bodhisattva. This was not to say that my other Tibetan teachers were not Bodhisattvas, but I had known Dhardo Rimpoche longer than I had known any of them, had spent more time in his company, and in our odd mixture of Hindi, Tibetan, and English I had a serviceable medium of communication such as I did not have with any of them. He had never given me an outline of his biography, as Yogi Chen had done in his first talk to Khantipalo and me, but from the conversations we had had over the years I had come to know something about him. I knew that he had been born in Dhartsendo, in Eastern Tibet; that his father was a merchant; that at an early age he had entered Drepung Gompa, the great Gelug monastic university near Lhasa; that he had passed all his examinations with great credit; that his teacher was strict but kind; that a breakdown in his health had prevented him from completing his studies at the Tantric College, where the routine was demanding and conditions harsh; that in 1947, at the age of twenty-nine, he had come to India in search of health; and that on his return, after he had been back only eighteen months, the Dalai Lama's government had appointed him abbot of the Tibetan monastery at Bodh Gaya, thus obliging him to make the long and arduous journey to India for the second time.

It was at Bodh Gaya, in 1949, that our paths had first crossed (though I did not know this at the time), when looking out of the window of his room Dhardo Rimpoche saw me standing on the flat roof of the Maha Bodhi rest house nearby. Since then we had met, had become friends, and had worked together for the good of Buddhism in various ways, so that I was more than compensated for the disappointments I had suffered at the hands of those who in my early years in Kalimpong were supposedly working with me. In 1956, the year of the 2500th Buddha Jayanti, Dhardo Rimpoche and I toured the principal Buddhist holy places as guests of the Government of India. This marked a definite stage in the development of our friendship. In the course of the tour I got to know the Rimpoche better, and the better I knew him the more I liked and respected him. I saw how unassuming he was, how kind, and how mindful in everything he did. Later, in Kalimpong, I had many opportunities, over the years, of observing his great and noble qualities. I saw how helpful he was to visiting Western scholars, how utterly devoted to the welfare of the pupils of his school, how patient with his irascible old mother, and how independent in his dealings with Tibetan officials, most of whom expected from other Tibetans only subservience. In short, Dhardo Rimpoche manifested in his life to a high degree the 'perfections' (*paramitas*) of generosity (*dana*), ethics (*shila*), patience (*kshanti*), energy (*virya*), concentration (*samadhi*), and wisdom (*prajna*), the practice of which for the benefit of all beings made one a Bodhisattva, and I rejoiced at my good fortune in being able to receive the Bodhisattva ordination from such a person.

The ordination took place at the Old Bhutan Palace. I do not remember the details of the ceremony, which was in Tibetan, but I do recollect having a strong sense of the Rimpoche's presence on his throne in front of me and of Khantipalo's presence at my side, as well as a strong sense of there being a bond between the three of us. After the ceremony, I felt I was no longer merely an admirer of the Bodhisattva ideal. I was now committed to the realization of that ideal in my own life. In other words, I had been formally enrolled as a member of the Mahayana sangha. This did not mean that I had abandoned the Hinayana, into one of whose schools I had been ordained as a monk, but only that the Hinayana had been integrated into the much wider context of the Mahayana. Indeed, it was one of the Bodhisattva precepts (*samvara-shila*) that the Bodhisattva should refrain from disparaging the Hinayana. Dhardo Rimpoche later went through the precepts with me, explaining the eighteen major and forty-six minor precepts, and helped me to make an English version of them. I sent a copy of this version to Khantipalo, who was then in Bangkok.

While he was still in Kalimpong, there took place the second of the two events that were of special significance to us both. This was the ceremonial planting of the bodhi tree sapling he had brought with him from Bodh Gaya, where it had been grown from seed by the monks of the Thai temple. The planting formed part of the Vihara's celebration of Shaga Dawa, the anniversary of the Buddha's Enlightenment according to the Tibetan calendar. I wielded the spade, while Khantipalo firmed the roots of the sapling, which was about two feet high, and filled in the hole. Despite the poverty of the soil, it flourished.

Chapter Fourteen

HINDI-CHEENI BHAI-BHAI

On 23 October 1962, the Government and people of India experienced a rude awakening from a dream – the dream of *Hindi-Cheeni bhai-bhai* or 'Indians and Chinese are brothers'. The awakening came when well-equipped Chinese troops crossed, without warning, the border between north-east India and Tibet. They crossed it in force, and eventually attacked along the whole 550-mile border. At a number of points their advance units made deep incursions into Indian territory, routing the Indian troops, taking many prisoners, and causing a mass exodus of the local people, most of whom were tribals. It was not until 1963, after a meeting between the Indian and Chinese prime ministers, that the invaders withdrew to the McMahon Line, as the *de facto* boundary between India and Tibet was known. By that time, Indian public opinion had turned against the peddlers of the *Hindi-Cheeni bhai-bhai* dream, which had lulled the country into a state of complacency and unpreparedness.

I was in Kalimpong at the time, having decided to suspend my preaching tours in the plains for a year or two, and at first I heard only rumours of fighting in the north-east, five or six hundred miles away. There had been such rumours before, but nothing had come of them, and like the rest of Kalimpong I saw no cause for concern. I realized that the situation was a serious one only when I awoke one morning to find that during the night the whole Chinese community had been arrested and taken away. Some of them were shopkeepers, and the next time I walked through the bazaar I saw that the authorities had boarded up their shops in order to prevent looting. How many Chinese had been living in Kalimpong I did not know. There may have been a hundred of them, or even two hundred. In any case, there were enough children for them to have needed a Chinese-language school. During my early months in Kalimpong, I had visited the school more than once and had got to know the tall, thin headmaster, a Mr Shen, who was an artist, and who made a series of ink drawings in traditional Chinese style for an illustrated edition of my poems that I was hoping to bring out. He was later replaced by a nominee of Peking, and I gathered that there had been a struggle between the Nationalist and Communist factions within the community for control of the school. As it happened, the majority of the town's Chinese inhabitants were Nationalists, but this had not prevented the Government from arresting and removing the whole community, probably out of fear that they might act as a fifth column. The only Chinese person not to be arrested and removed that night was Yogi Chen, who probably was spared either because he was a holy man or on account of his well-known antipathy to Communism.

The situation was indeed a serious one, as the drastic nature of the action taken against Kalimpong's Chinese community suggested, and it became more serious every day; even every hour. Every day brought news of fresh defeats suffered by the Indian Army and of further advances by the invading Chinese. The Chinese troops seemed to be irresistible, and people began to wonder how deep into Indian territory they intended to penetrate. Soon it was rumoured that their objective was Kalimpong, for had not Peking Radio denounced Kalimpong as the place where reactionary Tibetan aristocrats and imperialist American agents conspired against the Tibetan people and their Chinese friends? Later it was rumoured that the objective was not Kalimpong but Teesta Bridge, which was of obvious strategic importance. But this was almost immediately superseded by another rumour, to the effect that the objective was Siliguri, the nearest railhead. Finally it was rumoured that the ultimate objective of the invasion was Calcutta, the possession of which would give Chinese-occupied Tibet access to the Bay of Bengal and the Indian Ocean.

As the rumours became ever more alarming, something like panic began to be felt in the town, at least in some quarters. The potential fifth column had already been rounded up and taken, as I afterwards learned, to an internment camp in Dehra Dun, and now Government officials started sending their families away to the safety of the plains. Some of the yellow-turbaned Marwari merchants did likewise, while middle-class Bengalis who had been spending the traditional Hindu holiday season in Kalimpong thought it prudent to return to Calcutta. The Kazini, who seemed to hear every rumour that was afloat, and who scanned the newspapers with even more than her usual intensity, was convinced that the Chinese troops had Kalimpong in their sights and that nothing could stop them reaching the town. She and the Kazi had a jeep and a driver on standby all the time, she told me, in case they had to leave in a hurry. The jeep was stocked with provisions, and there would be room in it for me. We would escape by way of the track which ran past the Vihara down to the Lepcha village of Chebo Busti and thence to the Duars, thus avoiding Teesta Bridge, which would surely be blown up by the Indian Army to prevent the Chinese pushing further south. Though the Kazi acquiesced in his wife's plans for a dramatic, last-minute escape, he appeared to think they were in no real danger. The Kazini strongly suspected that the reason for his equanimity was that through secret channels of his own he was in contact with the Chinese and had come to some kind of understanding with them. But though she more than once questioned him on the subject, the enigmatic Kazi would neither affirm nor deny that this was the case. He would only laugh and rub his hands together.

The authorities must have been concerned lest there should be a mass exodus from Kalimpong, as there had been from towns and villages further east. This would create its own problems, and one morning I received a visit from Inspector Mukherjee, the Frontier Officer, who was in charge of the Foreigners Registration Office, to which all foreigners, including Tibetan refugees, had to report on their arrival in the town. I had had no official dealings with him, for I was a UK citizen, not a foreigner, but we had friends in common, and I knew him fairly well. Like many of his colleagues he was corrupt, and was known to accept bribes from Tibetan refugees desperate to be allowed to stay in India. He was in uniform, and after we had chatted for a few minutes he told me that he had just been with the Subdivisional Officer and that the latter had two requests to make of me. The first was that I should not leave Kalimpong, and he would be conveying a similar request to Dhardo Rimpoche. The Rimpoche and I were highly respected by the people of Kalimpong, and if we left many of them would follow our example, thinking that we could be trusted to know whether or not it was safe to remain. I had no thought of leaving, any more than Dhardo Rimpoche had, and I told Mukherjee as much. What I did not tell him was that even if Dhardo Rimpoche and I were to leave Kalimpong, our departure would not in my opinion be the signal for a general exodus as the authorities seemed to believe. Government officials, Marwari merchants, and holidaying Bengalis might fear the approach of the Chinese Communist troops, but the bulk of the population, which was ethnically Nepalese, regarded it with a degree of equanimity. The truth of the matter was that the Government officials, the Marwaris, and the Bengalis, all came from the plains, and that many hill people saw them – and often experienced them – not as fellow citizens of India but as oppressors and exploiters, and therefore tended to look upon the Chinese as liberators. For them it was not 'Indians and Chinese are brothers' but 'Hillmen and Chinese are brothers'.

'*You* are slit-eyed; *we* are slit-eyed,' Chinese agents had for years been telling the peasants and tea garden labourers of the area. 'We are from the same stock. We are brothers.' And the lesson had sunk in.

The SDO's second request was that I should organize a spontaneous demonstration against China's unprovoked attack on India. The Deputy Commissioner had telephoned the SDO, Mukherjee confided. There had been a spontaneous demonstration in Darjeeling, he had told him. Why had there not been one in Kalimpong? The speakers at the demonstration should say that the territory invaded by the Chinese troops was definitely part of India, Mukherjee warned me, and that China had definitely committed an act of aggression. It was particularly important that the word 'aggression' should be used. I found nothing to cavil at in this, and lost no time in going to see Dhardo Rimpoche and inviting him to speak at the demonstration, which I had decided should take the form of a public meeting at the Town Hall. I also invited other prominent citizens to speak, hired the Town Hall, and arranged for the meeting to be announced by beat of drum throughout the bazaar.

When the day came, the Town Hall was packed to capacity, and I was glad that I had arranged for loudspeakers to relay the proceedings to the crowds gathered outside. Dhardo Rimpoche and I were the principal speakers, he in Tibetan and I in English. Of the other speakers, two of them spoke in Nepali and one in Hindi. I saw to it that Dhardo Rimpoche was allowed more time than anyone else, for, as I had expected would be the case, the audience consisted mainly of Tibetans, most of whom understood only their own language. Neither the Rimpoche nor I felt any qualms about heeding Mukherjee's warning. China had invaded territory that was definitely part of India, we declared, and therefore China had definitely committed an act of aggression.

Years later I discovered that there was another side to the story, and that the situation was not quite so straightforward as I had been led to believe. At the Simla Conference of 1913 (according to the *Encyclopaedia Britannica*) the representatives of Great Britain, China, and Tibet had agreed that the McMahon Line should be accepted as marking the boundary between north-east India and Tibet. Two days later, however, the Chinese republican government disavowed its plenipotentiary and refused to sign a covenant. After the independence of India in 1947, Communist China made claims to a huge swathe of territory south of the McMahon line, on the grounds that the boundary had never been recognized by China and was the result of British aggression. Some maps showed the disputed territory as Chinese, some showed it as part of India, and some as part of Tibet.

From declaring that China had committed an act of aggression against India, it was only a short step to denouncing China for invading and occupying Tibet, and it was a step that neither Dhardo Rimpoche nor I hesitated to take. Both condemned, in the strongest terms, the barbarous behaviour of the invaders. We condemned the destruction of monasteries, the torture and killing of monks, the desecration of sacred books and images, the brutal suppression of the Lhasa uprising of 1959, and the virtual enslavement of the entire Tibetan people. In the heady days of *Hindi-Cheeni bhai-bhai* it would have been difficult to speak in this way at a public meeting. Communists and fellow travellers, whether Indian or Nepalese, would have denounced one as a warmonger or an American agent, and probably no Tibetan refugee would have dared to attend. But the situation had changed dramatically, and now Dhardo Rimpoche and I were free to speak our minds. In the course of my own speech I was unable to resist the temptation to refer in a rather pointed fashion to the change that had taken place. When the Chinese invaded Tibet we were not allowed to talk of aggression, I said, but now that China has invaded *India*.... I did not need to complete the sentence, which in any case was interrupted by laughter and applause by those who understood English. Whether Dhardo Rimpoche made a similar allusion I do not know, but from the expression on the faces of his Tibetan auditors I could tell that what he was saying was very much to their liking.

Over the years, Dhardo Rimpoche had developed into a very good public speaker, admittedly with the help of a little coaching from me. In Tibet there was no tradition of public speaking, or of lecturing, in the Western sense, though learned lamas might sometimes give expositions of particular sacred texts. The lack of such a tradition in the old Tibet was glaringly obvious at the Tsongkhapa death anniversary meeting I organized, which was attended by many eminent lamas. One of the speakers was Dudjom Rimpoche, but he spoke, or rather read from a prepared text, in a kind of rapid whisper which was audible only to those who were sitting in the front row of the auditorium. According to Tibetan notions of etiquette, by speaking in this way one showed respect for one's auditor or auditors, and Dudjom Rimpoche was known for his refined, aristocratic manners. By contrast, Dhardo Rimpoche had mastered the art of public speaking as this was understood in the West. Not only did he speak loudly and clearly; he spoke with vigour, and he dealt in a simple, straightforward manner with such matters – whether secular or religious – as were of serious concern to his audience. The Tibetans of Kalimpong had come to look forward to the Rimpoche's speeches. They attended in large numbers whenever he gave one, and listened with close attention.

This was very much the case on the day of our 'spontaneous demonstration', as Dhardo Rimpoche denounced China for invading and occupying Tibet and condemned the barbarous behaviour of its troops. Not that he spoke only in this vein. From condemning the Chinese he soon passed to exhorting the Tibetans, or at least those Tibetans who filled the Town Hall and who were gathered outside. He urged them to preserve their culture, to practise their religion, to make sure that their children learned Tibetan, to live peaceably in India, which had given them a refuge from the oppressive rule of the Chinese, and not to give up hope that Tibet would one day be free again. Above all, he urged them not to quarrel among themselves, but to live in unity.

Though I understood very little Tibetan, it was not difficult for me to catch the drift of Dhardo Rimpoche's speech. Not only did I have a good idea what he was going to say; I was familiar with his manner of speaking, and I could follow the changing expressions on the faces of his hearers as grief gave way to resignation, resignation to confidence, and confidence to hope. At that time, the Tibetans of Kalimpong were in need of hope, especially the refugees, who were very much in the majority. They had heard with increasing dismay of China's invasion of Indian territory, of the steady advance of the Chinese troops, and that – as it was rumoured – the objective of those troops was Kalimpong. Having escaped from Tibet with so much difficulty, would they be forced to flee from the Chinese a second time? In the circumstances it was natural that some of them should turn for guidance and encouragement not only to the spiritual leaders, such as Dhardo Rimpoche, but also to a certain class of gods. These were the gods who, when ritually invoked by a qualified person, would deliver a message, or answer a question, through the mouth of a medium while the latter was in a state of trance. Their utterances were taken down by an amanuensis and printed from wood blocks. There were several such oracles in circulation among the Tibetans of Kalimpong. One of them came into my hands, and with Prajnaloka's help I made an English version of it. The second half of the oracle ran as follows.

> The position of the East Red Pig will not last long, but will vanish like a rainbow. Then a change will take place, and the Pig's harvest will be devoured by the Dog. The angry Tiger of the South is lying on the border. After a time the great storm of delusion will come, so don't believe it. The Snake and the Frog of the West will advance and withdraw in various ways. They don't see that they themselves will be ruined. The Cobra of the North is stretching out two tongues. It is somewhat dangerous to all beings. The sufferings of our Chintamani of the Himalayas will become clear like the sun.

The sufferings of 'our Chintamani of the Himalayas' (the Dalai Lama) may or may not have become clear as the sun, but there was no doubt that there was a change in the position of the East Red Pig. On 21 November, as suddenly and unexpectedly as they had crossed the McMahon Line a month earlier, the Chinese forces declared a unilateral ceasefire. Though it would be some months before they disappeared like a rainbow, the conflict was definitely at an end. Or rather, the invasion was at an end, for the Indian Army had put up so ineffective a resistance that a conflict could hardly be said to have taken place. At the time of the ceasefire, the Chinese were in a very strong position. Having overrun an area more than half the size of England, they could easily have continued their advance and threatened, within a matter of days, the entire Assam Valley. Why, then, had they not done so? No one seemed to know, and in the absence of knowledge, speculation flourished. Some people were of the opinion that the Chinese wanted to give the world an example of magnanimity in victory; others thought they were concerned lest the winter snows should block the high Himalayan passes, interrupting their supply lines and making it impossible for them to return to Tibet until the following year. There was also the theory that the invasion was China's way of nudging a reluctant India towards the negotiating table and to a discussion of the territories in dispute between them in both the north-east and the north-west.

There was perhaps an element of truth in all these speculations. My own view was that the Chinese had come to resent India's assumption that it was the natural leader of Asia, and the invasion was meant to remind India that within the continent there was a power no less important than itself. The reason why the Chinese troops had not continued their advance was that they had made their point. *Hindi-Cheeni bhai-bhai* did *not* mean that India was the big brother and China the little brother.

Chapter Fifteen

INITIATION, AND AN INVITATION

The Bhutanese Gompa was situated not far from the Old Bhutan Palace, and like the latter it must have been built a hundred or more years ago, when Kalimpong was still part of Bhutan. A square, solid-looking structure with a corrugated iron roof, the gompa stood flanked by a few dark pines in the middle of its modest compound, which was surrounded by a low stone wall. The place had a deserted, neglected look. Except for the caretaker, who was rarely seen, it was unoccupied; nothing ever happened there, it seemed, and in the course of my years in Kalimpong I had only once been inside the shabby old building, the doors of which were kept firmly shut.

One day I heard that an incarnate lama was staying at the Bhutanese Gompa. I do not remember if his name was mentioned to me at the time, though even had it been mentioned it would then have meant very little to me. Since the newcomer was an incarnate lama, it was not long before I went to see him, taking Prajnaloka with me as my interpreter. We found the lama living not at the gompa but in a small cottage situated just inside the compound gate, to the right of the path leading to the gompa. As Prajnaloka explained the purpose of our visit, which was simply to pay our respects, I noticed that although the Rimpoche wore the maroon robe he had the long hair that betokened the lay tantric yogi. I noticed, also, that he was exceptionally tall, for despite his being seated cross-legged on his bed, his grey head bent over the Tibetan xylograph volume in his lap, this was immediately obvious. When his wife came in with the customary Tibetan tea she, too, turned out to be exceptionally tall, as did their two lanky grown-up daughters, who stood in the doorway for a few minutes regarding the visitors with undisguised curiosity. The average height of this family of giants must have been nearly six and a half feet. But the most remarkable thing about the Rimpoche himself was not his height but his smile, which was of extraordinary sweetness, without the least trace of sentimentality, and seemed to come from within, suffusing his soft features with a kind of glow.

How much I got to know about Dilgo Khyentse Rimpoche on that first visit I cannot say. Probably he told me that he and his wife and daughters had arrived in Kalimpong only recently, having escaped from Tibet to Bhutan, whence they had made their way to Sikkim. He would not have told me that he was – as I later discovered – one of the five tulkus of the great Jamyang Khyentse Wangpo, one of the leading figures in the Ri-me or 'Non-sectarian' movement in nineteenth-century Tibetan Buddhism, my own Jamyang Khyentse Rimpoche being also one of the five. He was therefore a very eminent lama indeed, and one who moreover was greatly revered by many people, especially those who were followers of the Kagyu and Nyingma traditions. Yet despite his being so eminent a lama, and so revered, it would have been difficult to find a more unassuming person than Dilgo Khyentse Rimpoche, or one who was more approachable. It was therefore not many months before I was visiting him regularly, accompanied sometimes by Prajnaloka and sometimes by Lobsang Norbu, for I never felt that I was being intrusive, or that I was wasting the Rimpoche's time. On the contrary, I felt that I was more than welcome. I always found the Rimpoche sitting crosslegged on his bed, a Tibetan xylograph volume in his lap. On my entering the tiny front room, he always looked up from his book with a little smile of recognition and pleasure, and his wife always came in after a few minutes with the Tibetan tea and, perhaps, some Tibetan bread. After a few such visits I observed that the Rimpoche never gave the impression of being disturbed or interrupted in what he was doing. His attention seemed to pass smoothly and seamlessly from one thing to another, as though all were equally interesting, equally important, and equally enjoyable, whether it was reading his book, answering a question from me, or drinking his tea.

It was no different when, on 9 May 1963, he transmitted to me the *phowa* or 'consciousness transference' of Amitabha, an oral tradition of the Nyingmapas. Once again I was able to observe how seamlessly his attention passed from one thing to another, passing on this occasion from whatever it was he had been doing before to the business of explaining to me the details of the practice and performing the simple ritual within whose context the transmission took place. The practice belonged to the Anuttarayoga Tantra, Khyentse Rimpoche told me. It was an oral tradition, having never been committed to writing, and was the simplest and easiest of all the phowa practices. It could be done anywhere and at any time but, for the time being at least, I was not to discuss it with anyone except Yogi Chen, though I was permitted to make notes for my personal use. Since the phowa included a visualization of Amitayus, the Buddha of Eternal Life, it was not necessary for me to do the long-life practice separately.

Though I was still visiting the Rimpoche regularly, it was not until 6 October that he visited the Vihara. Unfortunately, I have no recollection of this visit, though a note I made at the time informs me that we discussed the *Tharpe Delam*, one of the texts I had chanced to come across after receiving the Padmasambhava initiation from Kachu Rimpoche. The author of the *Tharpe Delam* was a celebrated Nyingma lama, Khyentse Rimpoche informed me, and the text itself was very well known among Nyingmapas. The work was written about 150 years ago, the author having died at the age of 87 in the early years of the reign of the Thirteenth Dalai Lama. The latter had once expressed his regret at not being able to meet the author, as he himself lived in Lhasa and the author in Kham.

Two weeks later, on 28 October, Khyentse Rimpoche initiated me into the sadhanas of Kurukulle, a dancing red dakini form of Tara, and Jambhala, the stout golden-yellow Bodhisattva of material wealth and spiritual riches. Like the phowa transmission, the ceremony took place in the Rimpoche's room in the cottage inside the Bhutanese Gompa's compound. Since there were only three of us, the third person being my interpreter, and since the smallness of the room obliged me to sit quite close to the guru, an atmosphere of intimacy prevailed. Indeed, it did not feel like a formal initiation at all. As on the occasion of the Amitabha phowa transmission, Khyentse Rimpoche resembled an affectionate father who was telling his son, quietly and confidentially, something that would be of immense value to him throughout his life.

Neither of the sadhanas required a full Tantric abhisheka, only a lesser initiation or special kind of blessing. I had asked for them at the instigation of Yogi Chen, who was overjoyed that the phowa transmission had given me a spiritual connection with the great Dilgo Khyentse Rimpoche and wanted me to strengthen the connection by taking further initiations from him. Kurukulle and Jambhala would help me in my work for the Dharma, he declared. Kurukulle belonged to the Lotus Family, of which Amitabha was the head. She embodied one of the four principal Buddha-activities, that of attraction or fascination, the three other activities being, respectively, those of maturation, pacification, and destruction. Jambhala belonged to the Jewel Family, the head of which was Ratnasambhava. There were three Jambhalas, Yogi Chen explained – the white, the yellow, and the black. The White Jambhala was a Buddha, the Yellow Jambhala a Bodhisattva of the eighth stage appearing in the form of a god, and the Black Jambhala a Dharmapala or Protector of the Dharma. The Yellow Jambhala was the main one, and it was *his* sadhana that Khyentse Rimpoche would give me if I asked. The Black Jambhala was hardly Buddhist, for he was worshipped for the acquisition of wealth by forcible means. When the Dalai Lama needed money he would get the Bon priests to worship the Black Jambhala on his behalf. The White Jambhala had a special connection with the Karmapa.

October 1963 was an important month for me as regards initiations, especially as in the course of it I also received an initiation from Dhardo Rimpoche. On 25 October he initiated me into the sadhana of Vaiduryaprabha or Blue Radiance, the blue-bodied Buddha of Healing, which like the Kurukulle and Jambhala sadhanas required only a lesser initiation or special kind of blessing. I had been drawn to the figure of the Medicine Buddha, as he was also called, after reading a translation of the Chinese version of the Mahayana sutra that bears his name. According to this popular scripture, prior to becoming a Buddha he had made twelve vows, and it was by virtue of these vows that those who worshipped him were guaranteed healing.

The fact that I was visiting Khyentse Rimpoche regularly, as well as Dhardo Rimpoche and Yogi Chen, meant that I often passed through the bazaar, on my way to or from the Bhutanese Gompa, or the Old Bhutan Palace, or the Five Leguminous Tree Hermitage. Nine months had passed since the withdrawal of the last Chinese troops from Indian territory, but signs of the alarm that the invasion had created were still to be seen. Chinese shops and business premises were still boarded up, and so far as anyone knew their unfortunate owners still languished in an internment camp or worse. But if there were no Chinese on the streets of Kalimpong, there were plenty of military personnel in their black berets and jungle greens. They came from the army camp which had been established at Rinkingpong, not far from the little Kagyu gompa and Dudjom Rimpoche's unfinished temple, both of which were now difficult of access. One day I happened to pass two *jawans*, as the ordinary soldiers were called, who like myself were on their way to the bazaar.

'We've got the atom bomb,' I heard one jawan say it to the other. 'If the Chinese give us any more trouble we'll drop it on Lhasa.'

India did not then have nuclear weapons, but the troops may have been told by their officers that she did have them in order to bolster their morale, which after their defeat at the hands of the Chinese was said to be very low.

But if Mother India did not have the atom bomb, she had plenty of other weapons. Gazing down the hillside from the Vihara garden I could make out, far below, the ant-like procession of trucks, artillery, and even tanks crawling along the road that zig-zagged its way from Teesta Bridge up to Kalimpong. As I discovered when I made an unscheduled flying visit to Darjeeling, Teesta Bridge itself was now protected by a battery of anti-aircraft guns, their barrels protruding disconcertingly from their half-camouflaged emplacement beside the road, and on both sides of the river there were swarms of green-clad jawans.

The flying visit was on account of Lobsang Norbu. At breakfast that morning I had been told that the Vihara's young manager had disappeared. Inquiries revealed that he and a good friend of his who worked at Arunachal had talked of joining the irregular force that Jigme Norbu, the Dalai Lama's eldest brother, was organizing for action against the Chinese troops in Tibet. According to Thubden, the two friends had probably gone to Darjeeling, where Jigme Norbu was based, in order to enlist. Even in the days of *Hindi-Cheeni bhai-bhai* there had been a surreptitious trickle of men and money from India to the legendary Khamba guerrillas, and now that India and China were no longer such good friends the operation could be carried on much more openly, albeit without the official sanction of the Indian government. Jigme Norbu's agents would travel round the area meeting young Tibetan men; they would talk to them about the importance of carrying on the armed struggle against the Chinese occupation, appeal to their patriotism, and, finally, assure them that if they volunteered they would be properly trained and equipped. Apparently Lobsang and his friend had been recruited in this way.

On arriving in Darjeeling I went straight from the motor stand to the Foreigners Registration Office, but no Lobsang Norbu had reported there, I was told. This left me wondering how best to continue my search for the runaway, and in the end I decided to consult a Bengali friend who had a watch repair shop on the main road into the town. I had not gone more than a hundred yards in that direction when I saw coming towards me through the crowd the familiar figure of Lobsang. He was not surprised to see me, nor was he surprised when I gave him a good scolding for having left the Vihara without telling me or anybody else that he was going, which was hardly in accordance with Tibetan good manners. That afternoon he accompanied me back to Kalimpong – and the Vihara. Though I admired the courage of the Khambas and other guerrillas, I believed that the cause for which they were fighting was a lost one, and I did not want to see Lobsang or any other young Tibetans sacrifice their lives for such a cause, however noble they might believe it to be. Lobsang later told me what he had learned about Jigme Norbu's force of irregulars. Those who volunteered to fight the Chinese were flown to a foreign country. He did not know the name of the country, but it was very far away, and the people there spoke English. The volunteers spent three months in that country. They were well treated, and were taught how to use rifles and other weapons. He did not know what happened to the volunteers once they had completed their training. No doubt some way was found of getting them into Tibet so that they could fight the Chinese.

When I repeated to the Kazini what Lobsang had told me, she expressed a degree of scepticism. She doubted if Jigme Norbu's guerrillas were trained in an English-speaking country. It was more likely, in her opinion, that the training took place at an American base where, of course, English would be spoken. The base was probably located somewhere in Pakistan. As I knew, the Kazini was more favourably disposed to Pakistan than to India, and the fact that it was cooperating with the Tibetan diaspora against Communist China would certainly have done it no harm in her eyes. Since the events of the previous year, she was more critical of India than ever, and would not have been sorry had her friend General Cariappa led a military coup against the corrupt and inefficient Congress government, as at one time it was rumoured he might. The Kazini was also tired of living in Kalimpong. The place had changed, she declared, and she would have left had she not been married to the Kazi and the Kazi not been married to his politics.

Kalimpong had indeed changed in the course of the last few years. The fresh influx of Tibetan refugees, the rumours of impending invasion by the Chinese, and the presence of troops and tanks on the streets, had all affected the atmosphere of the town. What was more, the authorities had become more suspicious of foreign visitors, especially Europeans and Americans, seemingly finding it difficult to believe that anybody could come to Kalimpong simply for the sake of the view. This meant that one's movements were watched, one's letters were intercepted and, though personally I had nothing to fear, I was glad that I now had a British passport.

I had not always had a passport. On my 'going forth' as a homeless wanderer on 18 August 1947 I had not only given away my worldly possessions, not only donned the traditional saffron robes of the world-renunciant. I had also destroyed my identification papers. Like the friend who went forth with me, I believed that nationalism was one of the greatest evils of the modern world, and that in becoming a homeless wanderer I had renounced not only all domestic ties and social obligations but all national loyalties as well. Believing this as I did, I had vowed never to admit to having any particular nationality. I was a citizen of the world!

It was not long before I found it impracticable to maintain, in all its youthful uncompromisingness, the attitude I had adopted. World citizens belonged to an ideal realm, not to the real world. Much as I might believe that I had no nationality, there were plenty of people –

not all of them officials – who believed I *did* have a nationality and wanted to know what it was. In the end, more than two years after my going forth, I wrote to the UK High Commissioner in New Delhi asking him to place my name on his Record of UK Citizens. This he did, giving me a serial number and requesting me to notify any change of address. For the next ten years his letter served me in lieu of a passport, and whenever I was required to give my passport number I gave my serial number on the High Commissioner's Record of Citizens. In 1962 I applied for a passport.

The reason I applied for one was that the English Sangha Trust had invited me to spend some time in England, and I had accepted the invitation. In accepting it I had made it clear that I would not be staying for more than four months, possibly six. At the time I saw myself as being permanently settled in India, which I had come to regard as my spiritual home. In Kalimpong, within sight of the snows, I had a peaceful hillside hermitage, the Triyana Vardhana Vihara, where I could meditate, study, write, and receive my friends, and from which I sallied forth on my preaching tours in the plains and to which, when I needed to recoup my energies, I could return. Above all, I had spiritual teachers of exceptional attainments, with most of whom I was in regular personal contact, and from whom I derived not just knowledge but inspiration. Thus there was little incentive for me to return to the land of my birth, much as I loved its language and its literature, and at first I was undecided whether or not to accept the Trust's invitation. Khantipalo was with me when it arrived, however, and when he pointed out that it was my duty to help spread the Dharma in England, inasmuch as I had been born and brought up there, I could not but recognize the force of his argument. I also reflected that the trip would enable me to see my parents and my sister, as well as to meet the various English Buddhists with whom I was in communication.

Between my acceptance of the English Sangha Trust's invitation and my departure from India there was an interval of two years. During this period the greater part of my time was spent meditating, or writing, or visiting such of my teachers as were in Kalimpong. I also went on a short preaching tour in the plains, leaving the Vihara in the care of Thien Chau, who was paying his annual visit to the hills. On my return some weeks later, I found that thieves had broken into my room the night before and that seven silver puja bowls were missing from my personal shrine. Thien Chau, Lobsang, and Thubden were asleep at the time and had heard nothing. When I told the Kazi and Kazini what had happened the Kazini was horrified, but the Kazi took a more philosophic – and more Buddhist – view of my loss. The robbery was a good omen, he assured me, especially as my life was about to enter on a new phase. It meant that a karmic debt had been paid and that I was now free to move forward without it hanging over my head.

Dhardo Rimpoche, too, was concerned that I was free to move forward. He was concerned, in particular, that I should not be held back by any threat to my life-force. Thus he had given me, not long before, the abhisheka of White Tara, the female Bodhisattva of Longevity, and with his help I had started making an English version of the text of the relevant sadhana. I wanted to complete a first draft of this version before leaving for England, and the Rimpoche and I spent many hours working on the project together. We worked in the evening, in the Rimpoche's quarters in the Old Bhutan Palace, and sometimes it seemed that there were three of us in the room, and that White Tara was looking down on our labours with a smile. We worked up to the very eve of my departure, so that when I packed my bag that night I was able to include the exercise book containing the completed draft.

The following morning the Kazi and Kazini arrived with their jeep, having offered to drive me down to Siliguri and see me onto my train. As we left the Vihara, a Nepalese woman carrying a churn of milk happened to cross the road directly in front of us. This was a very good omen, the Kazi announced happily. My trip was sure to be a success.

INDEX

The windhorse symbolizes the energy of the Enlightened mind carrying the truth of the Buddha's teachings to all corners of the world. On its back the windhorse bears three jewels: a brilliant gold jewel represents the Buddha, the ideal of Enlightenment, a sparkling blue jewel represents the teachings of the Buddha, the Dharma, and a glowing red jewel, the community of the Buddha's enlightened followers, the Sangha. Windhorse Publications, through the medium of books, similarly takes these three jewels out to the world.

Windhorse Publications is a Buddhist publishing house, staffed by practising Buddhists. We place great emphasis on producing books of high quality, accessible and relevant to those interested in Buddhism at whatever level. Drawing on the whole range of the Buddhist tradition, our books include translations of traditional texts, commentaries, books that make links with Western culture and ways of life, biographies of Buddhists, and works on meditation.

As a charitable institution we welcome donations to help us continue our work. We also welcome manuscripts on aspects of Buddhism or meditation. For orders and catalogues log on to www.windhorsepublications.com or contact:

Windhorse Publications	Perseus Distribution	Windhorse Books
11 Park Road	1094 Flex Drive	P O Box 574
Birmingham	Jackson, TN 38301	Newtown NSW 2042
B13 8AB	USA	Australia
UK		

Windhorse Publications is an arm of the Friends of the Western Buddhist Order, which has more than sixty centres on four continents. Through these centres, members of the Western Buddhist Order offer regular programmes of events for the general public and for more experienced students. These include meditation classes, public talks, study on Buddhist themes and texts, and bodywork classes such as t'ai chi, yoga, and massage. The FWBO also runs several retreat centres and the Karuna Trust, a fundraising charity that supports social welfare projects in the slums and villages of India.

Many FWBO centres have residential spiritual communities and ethical businesses associated with them. Arts activities are encouraged too, as is the development of strong bonds of friendship between people who share the same ideals. In this way the FWBO is developing a unique approach to Buddhism, not simply as a set of techniques, but as a creatively directed way of life for people living in the modern world.

If you would like more information about the FWBO please visit the website at www.fwbo.org or write to:

London Buddhist Centre	Aryaloka	Sydney Buddhist Centre
51 Roman Road	14 Heartwood Circle	24 Enmore Road
London	Newmarket	Sydney NSW 2042
E2 0HU	NH 03857	Australia
UK	USA	

ALSO FROM WINDHORSE PUBLICATIONS

Teachers of Enlightenment

The refuge tree of the Western Buddhist Order

by Kulananda

Out of the depths of a clear blue sky emerges a beautiful tree of white lotus flowers. On the tree are many figures – historical, mythical, and transcendental – each a teacher of Enlightenment. This is the Refuge Tree: a compelling image which, in its many different forms, has inspired Buddhists for centuries.

Kulananda explains the significance of the figures on the Refuge Tree of the Western Buddhist Order. These teachers, each in their own way, have all changed the world for the better, playing a part in the creation of the rich Buddhist tradition we know today.

304 pages, with illustrations and b&w photos
ISBN 1 899579 25 7
£12.99/$21.95/€21.95